Cascade method

PIANO THEORY

THIS BOOK BELONGS TO: ______________________________

Index

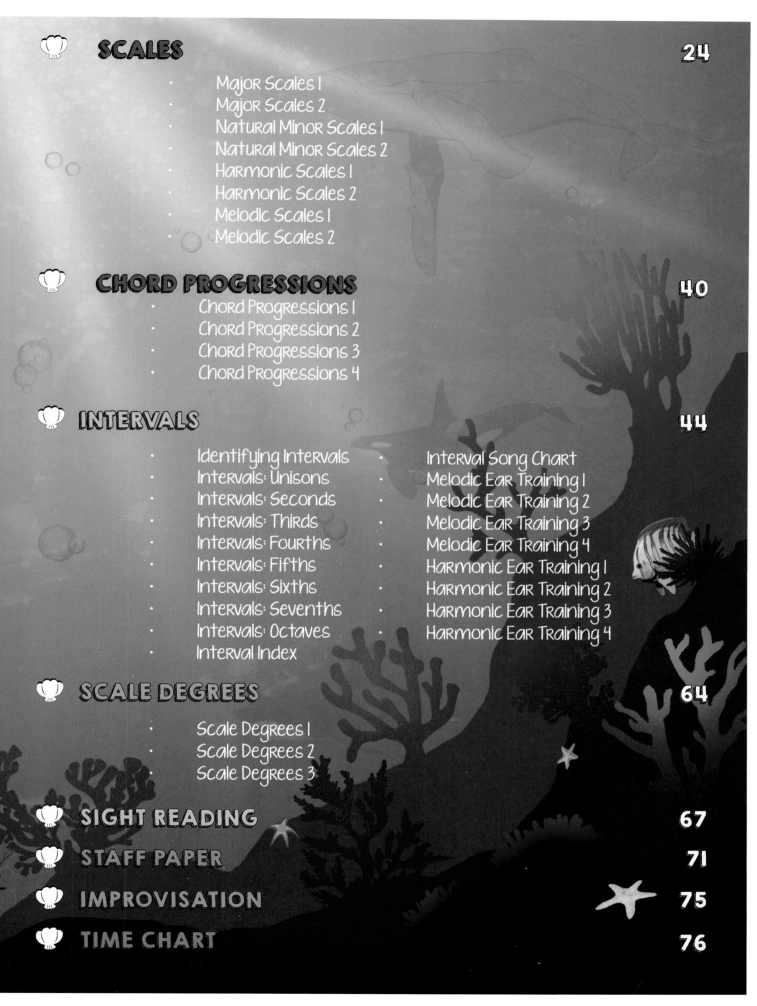

My Piano

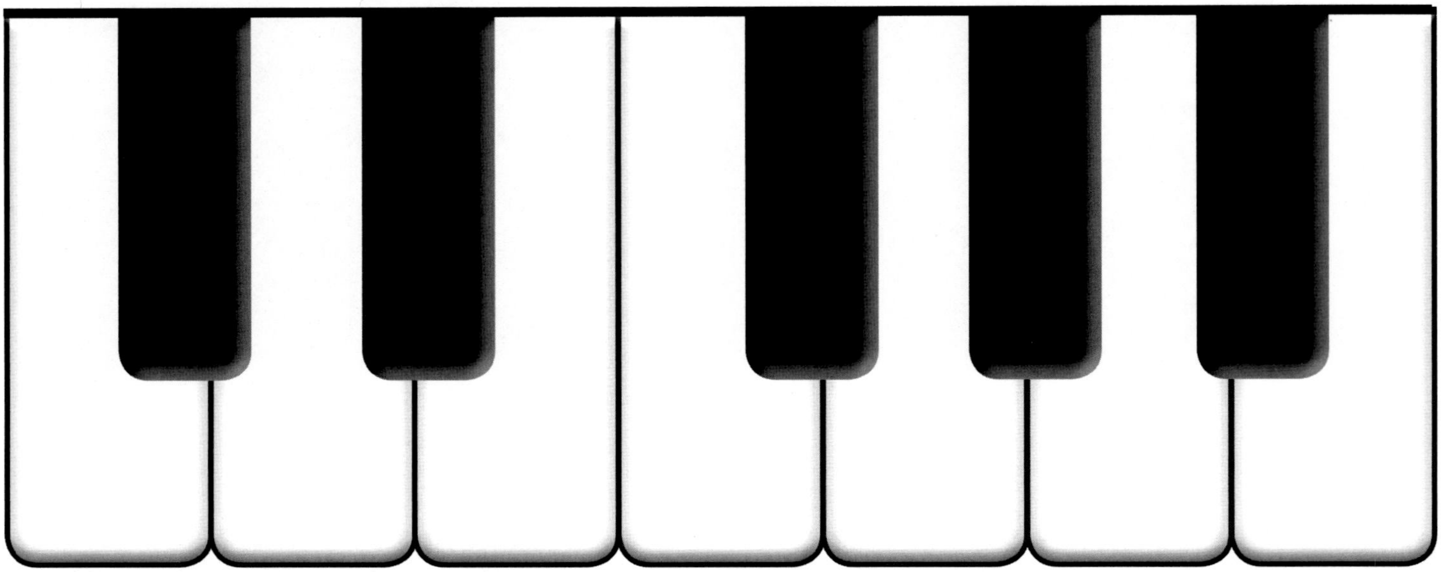

... has how many ...

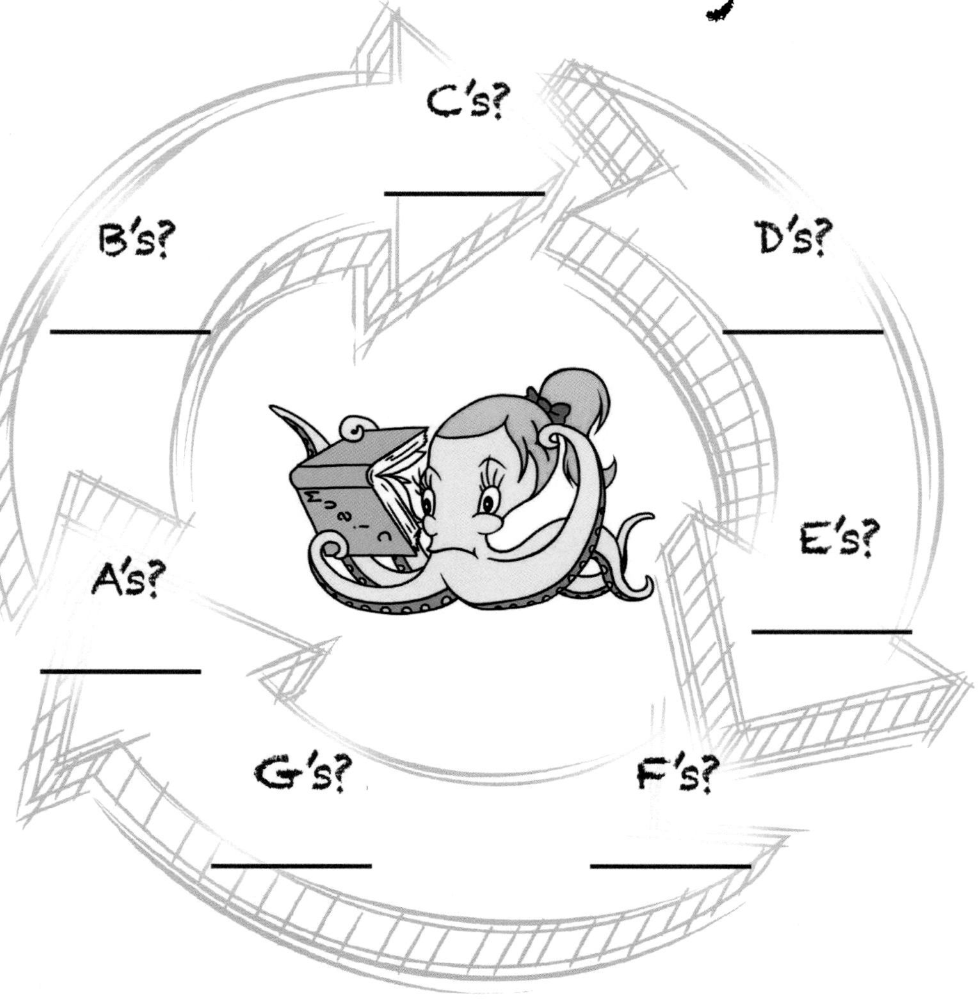

Note Dictionary

LINE NOTES

SPACE NOTES

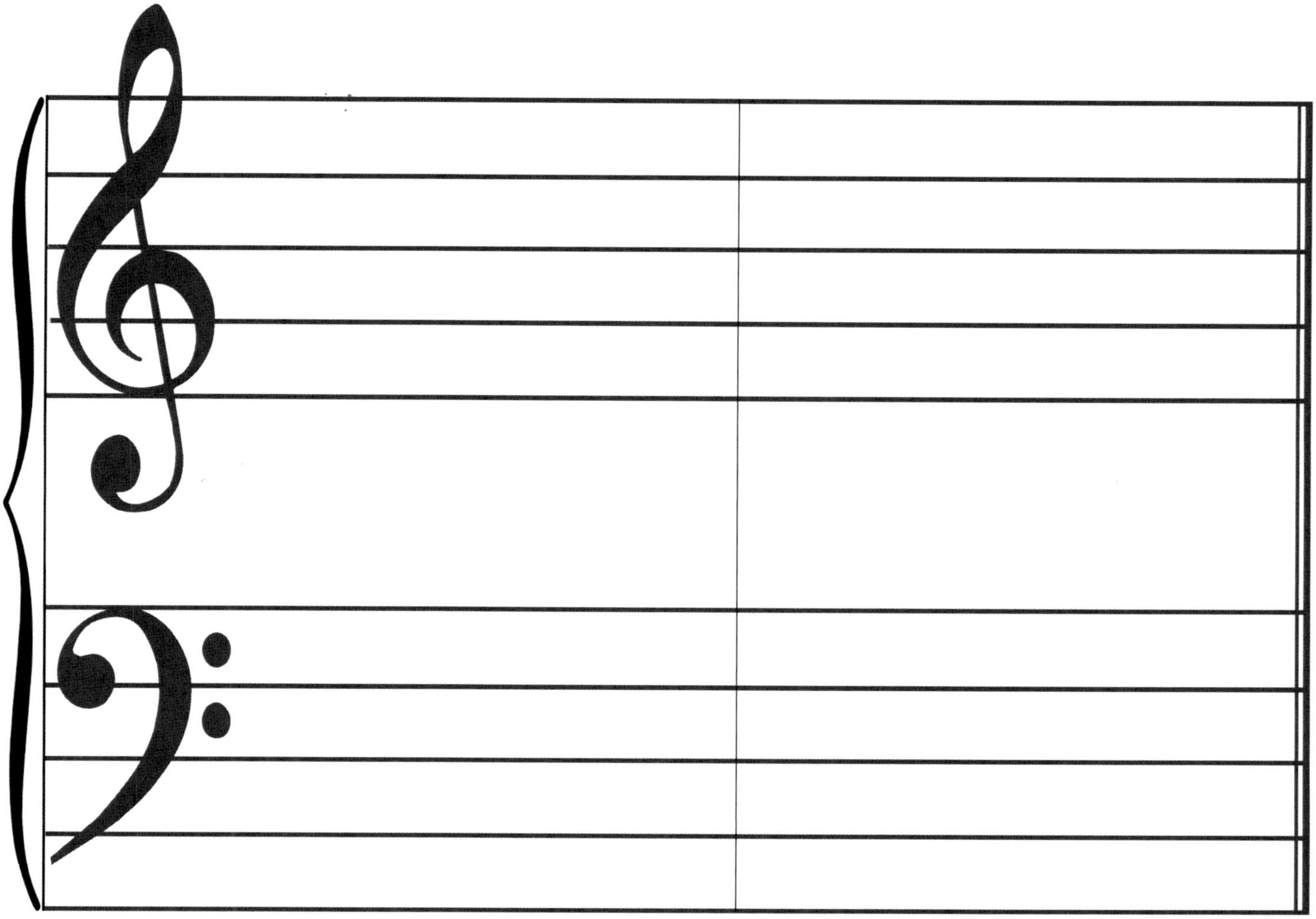

Staff Vocabulary

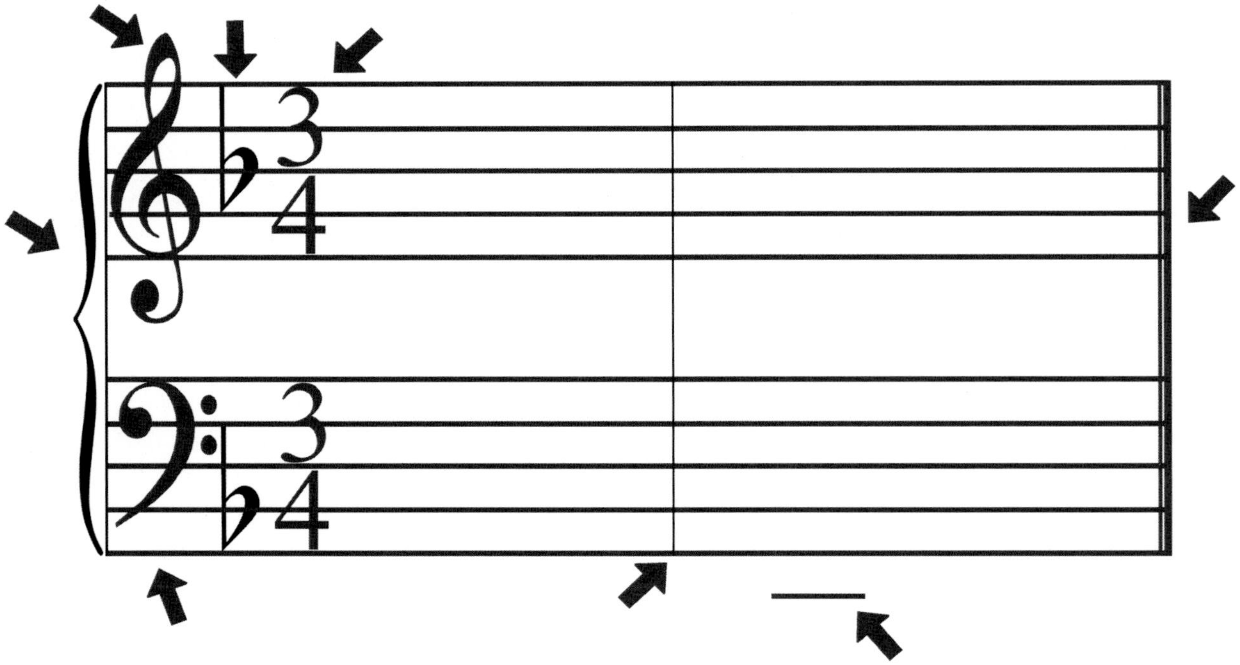

Tempo Chart

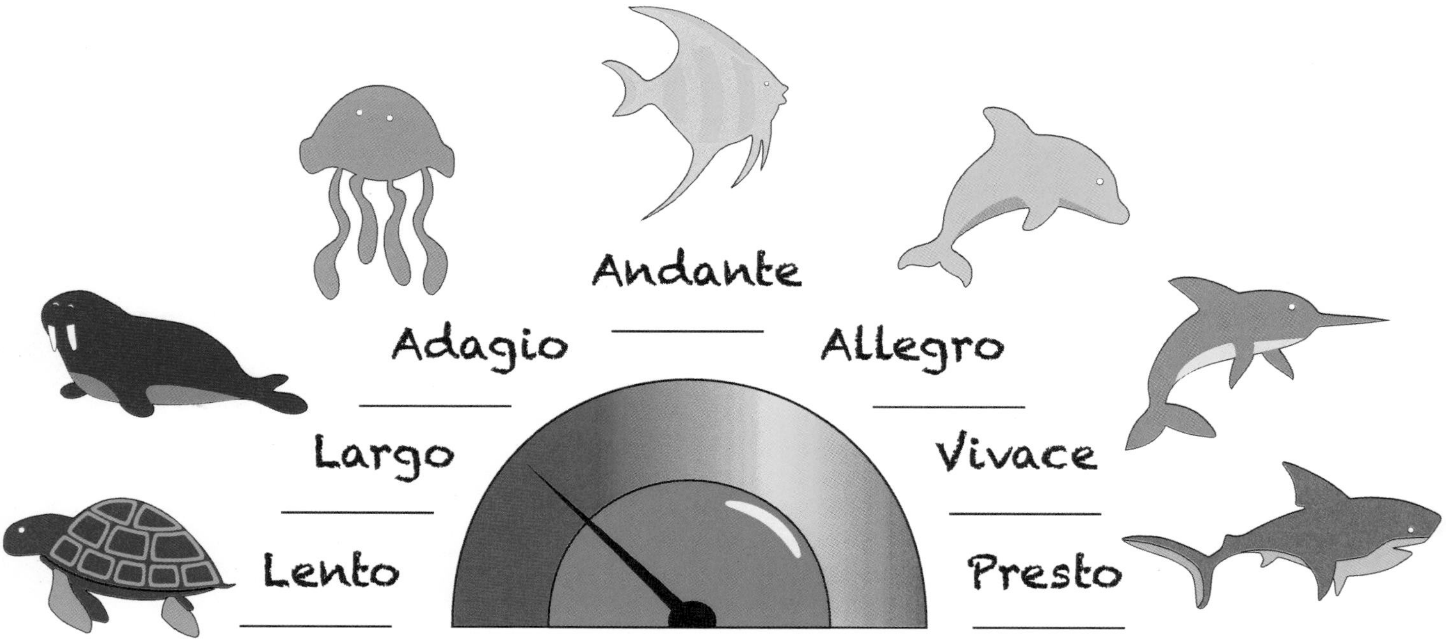

Musical Terms

- Time signature
- Key signature
- Treble clef
- Dynamics
- Composer
- Bass clef
- Staccato
- Tie
- Title
- Slur
- Accent
- Fermata
- Crescendo
- Decrescendo
- Ledger Line
- Phrase marking
- Dotted quarter note

- Bar line
- Measure
- Space note
- Eighth rest
- Whole note
- Eighth note
- Quarter note
- Grace note
- Line note
- Quarter rest
- Stress mark
- Staff bracket
- Grand staff
- Pedal marking
- Tempo marking
- Measure number
- Double bar line

Cascade

Tara O'Brien

Rhythm Chart

NOTES Name | Beat value | Syllable | Choose your own words!

RESTS Name | Beat value | Make up your own rhythms!

ex.

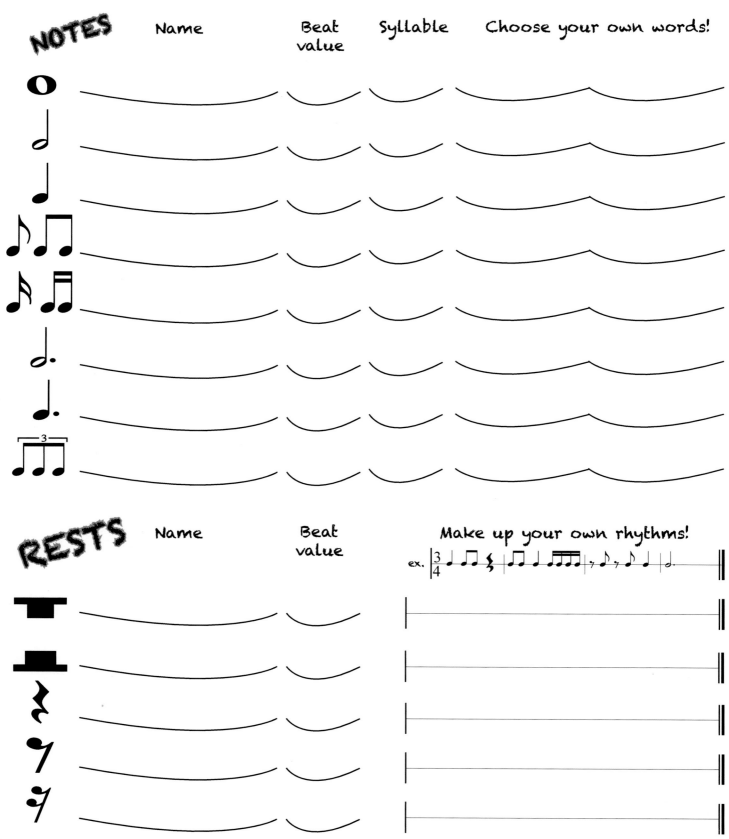

Dynamic Chart

Symbol	Name	Meaning
fff		
ff		
f		
mf		
mp		
p		
pp		
ppp		
<		
>		

Music Sentences

Fill in all the following:

Treble clef space notes:

____

Bass clef space notes:

____

Treble clef line notes:

____

Bass clef line notes:

____

Keys with sharps: ("how many sharps?")

____

Order of sharps: ("which sharps?")

____

Keys with flats: ("how many flats?")

____

Order of flats: ("which flats?")

____

Flash Cards : can you identify all the following?

- ◯ Treble clef notes
- ◯ Key signatures with sharps
- ◯ Bass clef notes
- ◯ Key signatures with flats

Circle of Fifths

down   up

b's   #'s

b's   #'s

b's   #'s

	How many?	Which ones?
#	Cars Get Dirty And Elephants Bake F#luffy C#akes	Fat Cats Go Dancing At Ella's Ball
b	Cute Fluffy Bbunnies Ebxplore Abnd Dbiscover Gbreen Cbabbage	BEAD Gum Candy Fruit

Chords 1: Triads

Root Position | Chord Rolls | Mega Chord Rolls

R.H. | L.H.

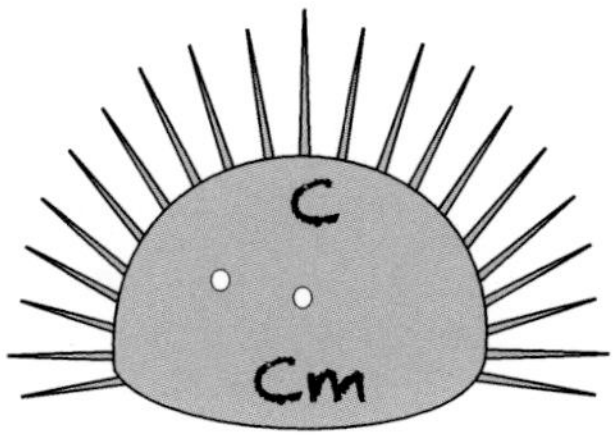

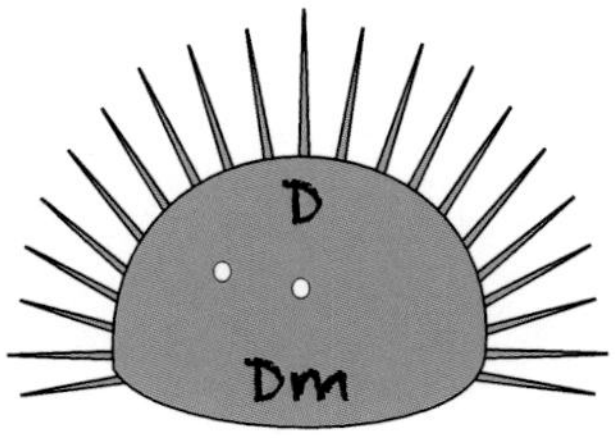

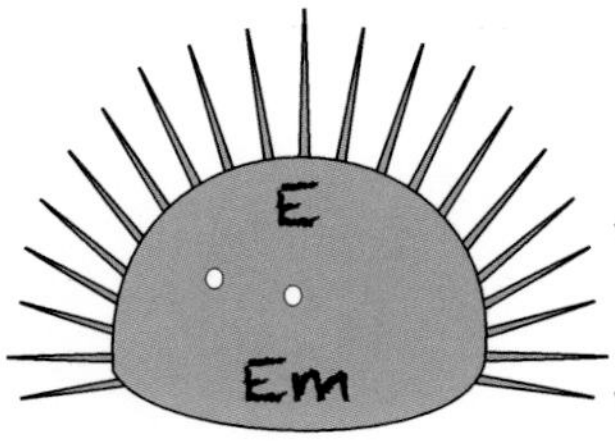

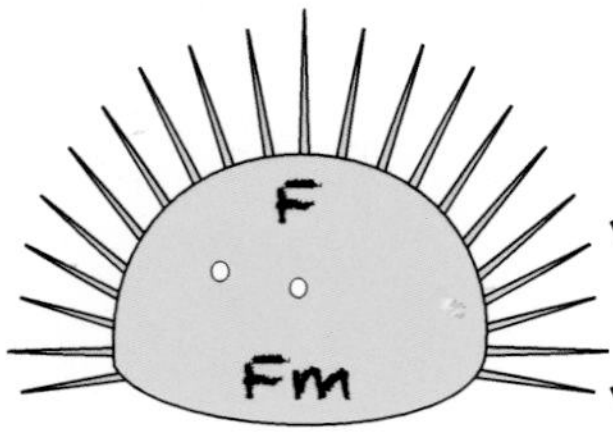

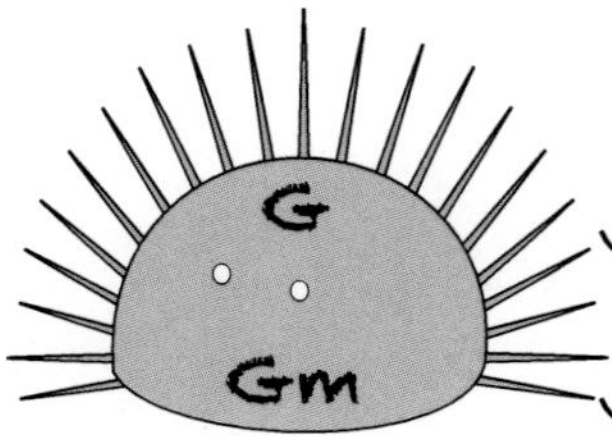

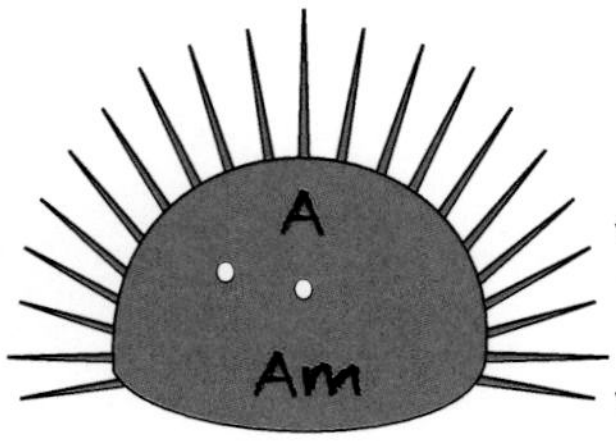

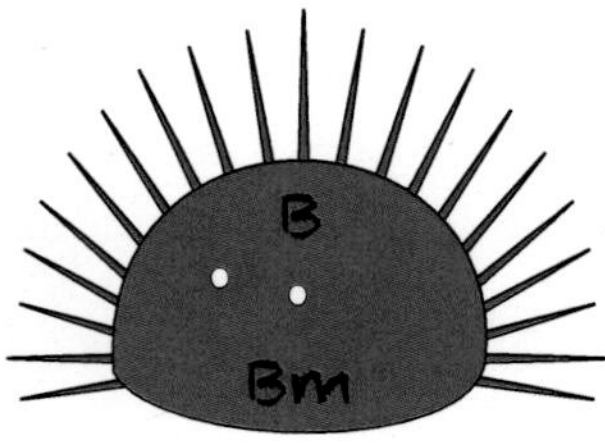

Chords 2: Triads

	Root Position R.H.	Root Position L.H.	Chord Rolls	Mega Chord Rolls
C#				
C#m				
Db				
Dbm				
D#m				
Eb				
Ebm				
F#				
F#m				
Gb				
G#				
G#m				
Ab				
Abm				
A#m				
Bb				
Bbm				

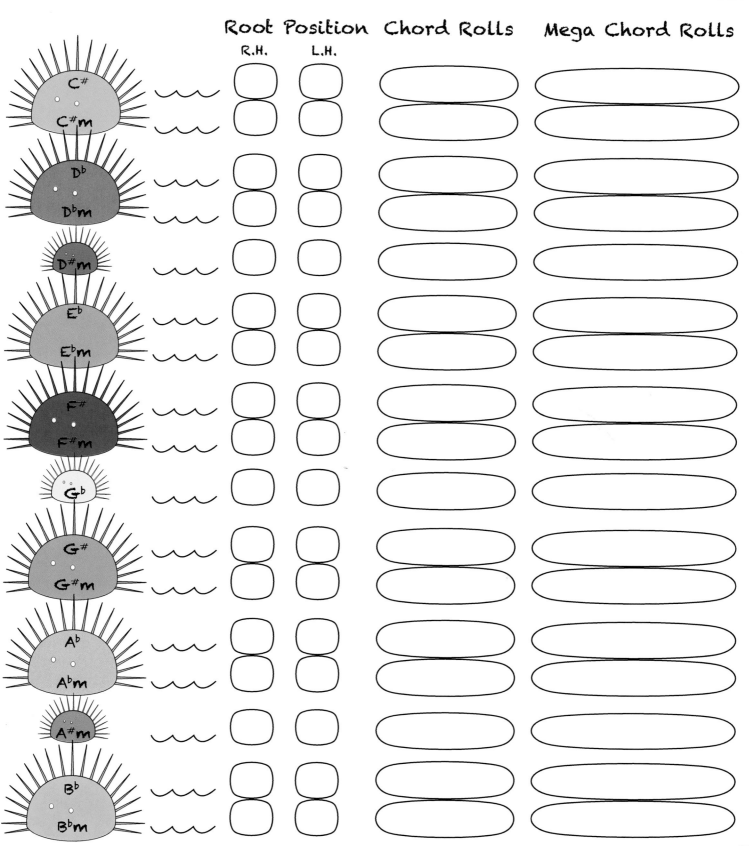

Chords 3: Triads

Chord Stealing — Up / Down

Chord Stealing — Up / Down

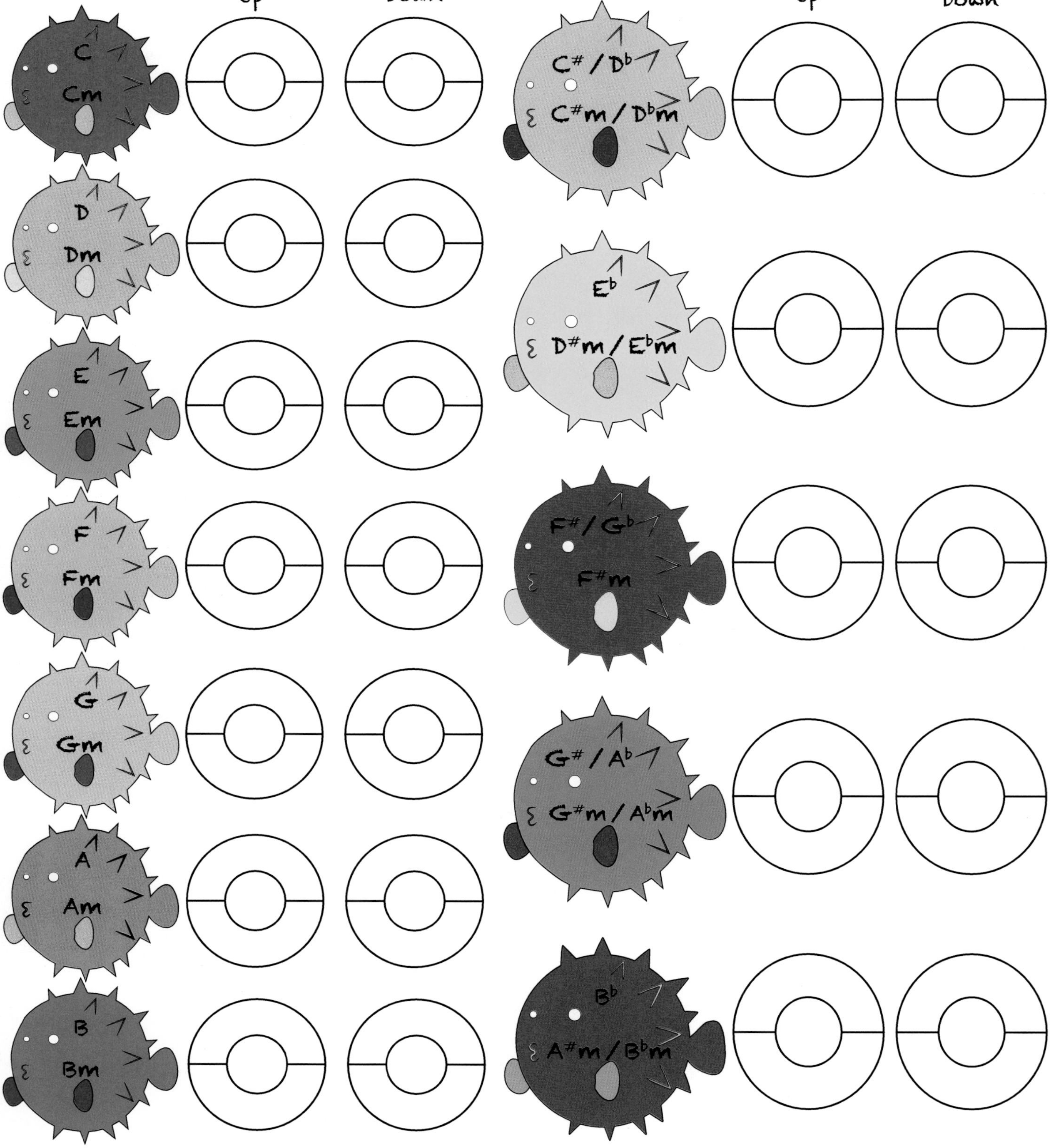

Chords 4

Use all 5 of your fingers on Root, Third, Fifth, Sixth, Octave

Note: Flat the 3rd and the 6th when playing the minor chords

	Blocked R.H.	Blocked L.H.	Rolled R.H.	Rolled L.H.
C				
D				
E				
F				
G				
A				
B				
C#				
Db				
Eb				
F#				
Gb				
Ab				
Bb				

	Blocked R.H.	Blocked L.H.	Rolled R.H.	Rolled L.H.
Cm				
Dm				
Em				
Fm				
Gm				
Am				
Bm				
C#m				
D#m				
Ebm				
F#m				
G#m				
Abm				
A#m				
Bbm				

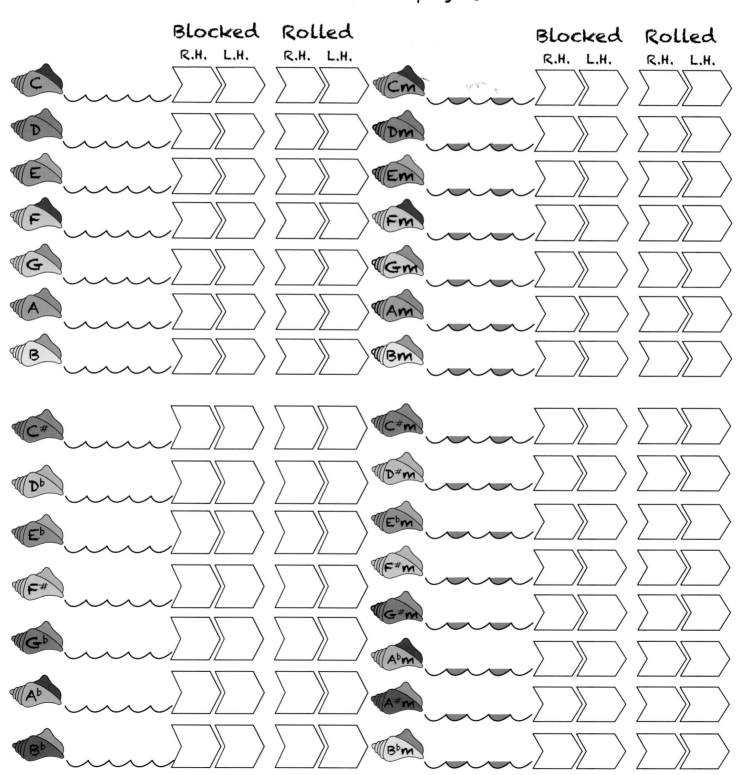

Chords 5

	Augmented	Diminished	Maj. Aug. Min. Dim.	Fully Diminished
C				
D				
E				
F				
G				
A				
B				
Chord Rolls				
Mega Chord Rolls				
Chord Stealing				

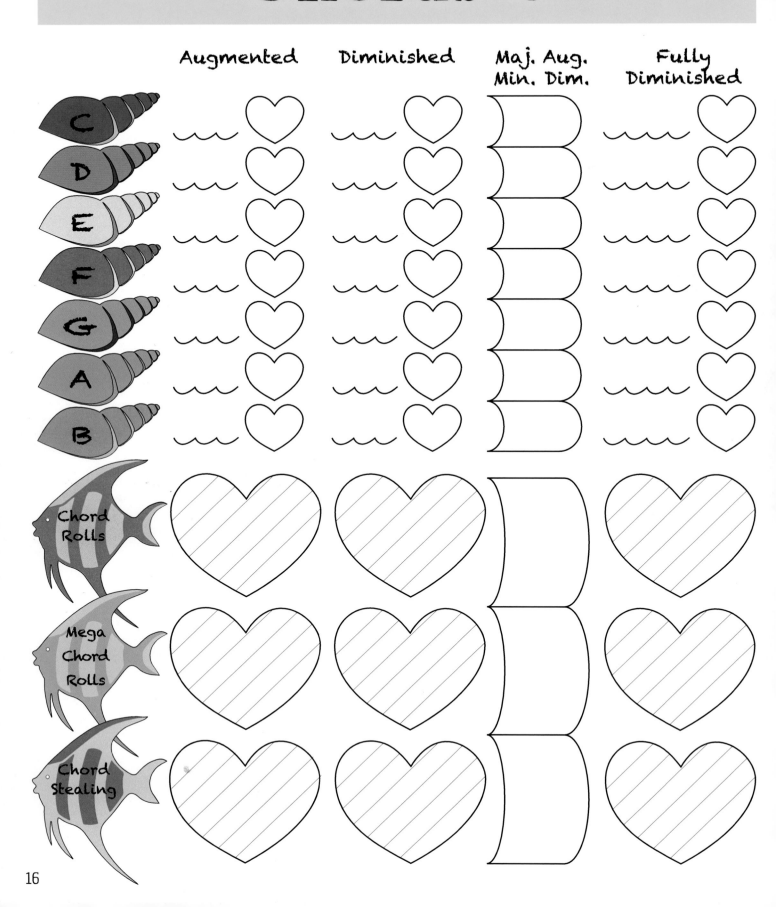

Chords 6

	Augmented	Diminished	Maj. Aug. Min. Dim.	Fully Diminished
C#/Db				
D#/Eb				
F#/Gb				
G#/Ab				
A#/Bb				
Chord Rolls				
Mega Chord Rolls				
Chord Stealing				

Seventh Chords 1

	Major 7th	Dominant 7th	Minor 7th	Minor Major 7th
	____ + __	____ + __	____ + __	____ + __
C				
D				
E				
F				
G				
A				
B				
Chord Rolls				
Mega Chord Rolls				
Chord Stealing				

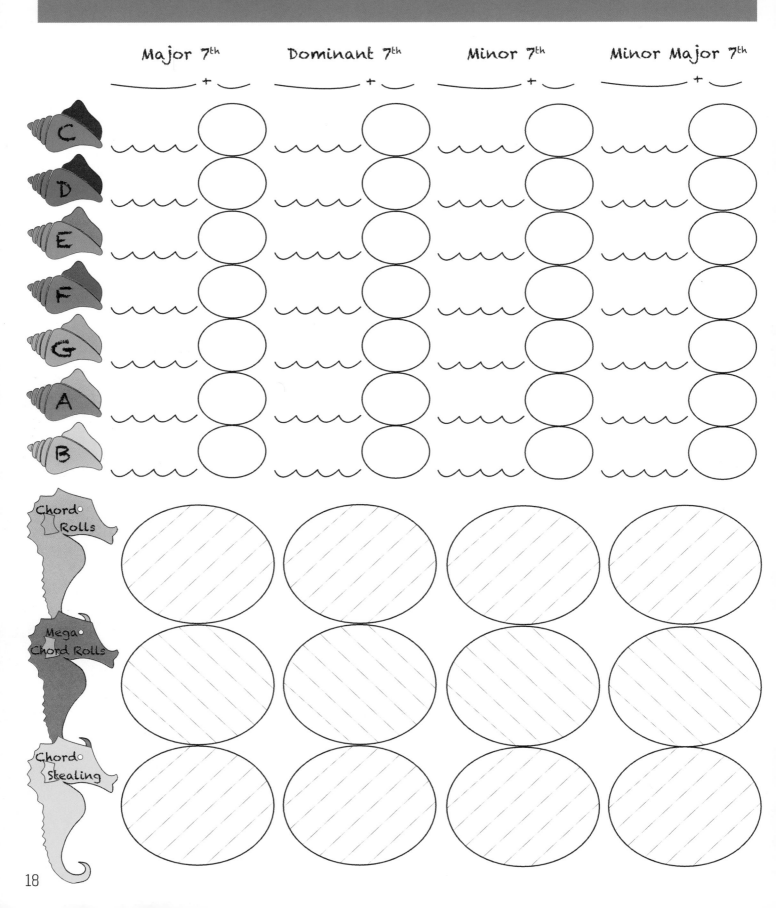

Seventh Chords 2

	Major 7th	Dominant 7th	Minor 7th	Minor Major 7th
	______ + ___	______ + ___	______ + ___	______ + ___
C# / Db				
D# / Eb				
F# / Gb				
G# / Ab				
A# / Bb				
Chord Rolls				
Mega Chord Rolls				
Chord Stealing				

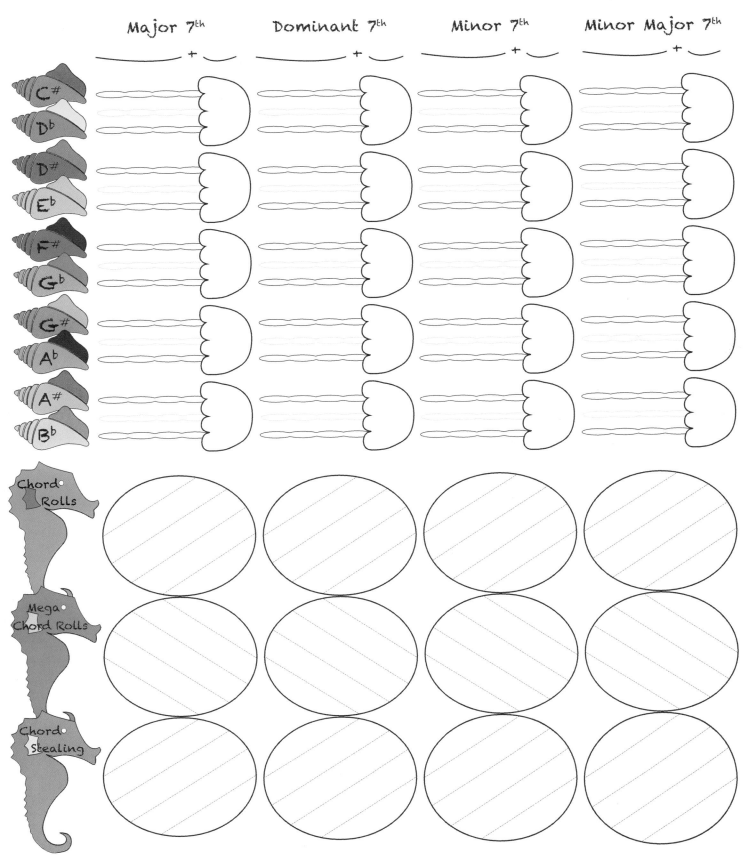

Inversions 1

	Root Position	1st Inversion	2nd Inversion	R.H.	L.H.
C major				☆	☆
C minor				☆	☆
D major				☆	☆
D minor				☆	☆
E major				☆	☆
E minor				☆	☆
F major				☆	☆
F minor				☆	☆
G major				☆	☆
G minor				☆	☆
A major				☆	☆
A minor				☆	☆
B major				☆	☆
B minor				☆	☆

Advanced Inversions 1

		Rolled	Both		Blocked	Both
C major	R.H.			R.H.		
	L.H.			L.H.		
C minor	R.H.			R.H.		
	L.H.			L.H.		
D major	R.H.			R.H.		
	L.H.			L.H.		
D minor	R.H.			R.H.		
	L.H.			L.H.		
E major	R.H.			R.H.		
	L.H.			L.H.		
E minor	R.H.			R.H.		
	L.H.			L.H.		
F major	R.H.			R.H.		
	L.H.			L.H.		
F minor	R.H.			R.H.		
	L.H.			L.H.		
G major	R.H.			R.H.		
	L.H.			L.H.		
G minor	R.H.			R.H.		
	L.H.			L.H.		
A major	R.H.			R.H.		
	L.H.			L.H.		
A minor	R.H.			R.H.		
	L.H.			L.H.		
B major	R.H.			R.H.		
	L.H.			L.H.		
B minor	R.H.			R.H.		
	L.H.			L.H.		

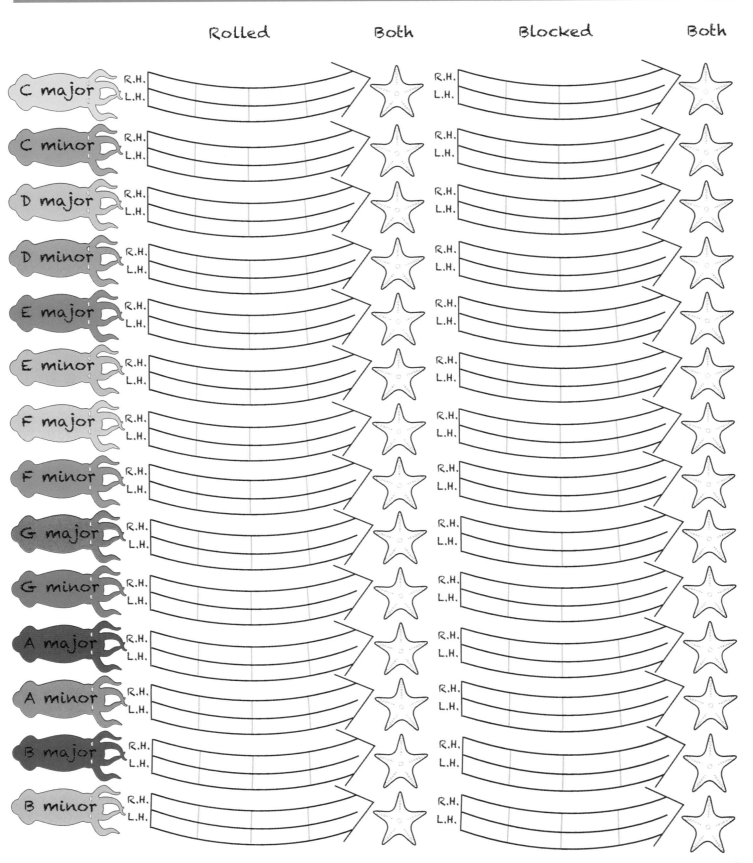

Inversions 2

	Root Position	1st Inversion	2nd Inversion	R.H.	L.H.
C# major				☆	☆
C# minor				☆	☆
Db major				☆	☆
Db minor				☆	☆
D# minor				☆	☆
Eb major				☆	☆
Eb minor				☆	☆
F# major				☆	☆
F# minor				☆	☆
Gb major				☆	☆
G# major				☆	☆
G# minor				☆	☆
Ab major				☆	☆
Ab minor				☆	☆
A# minor				☆	☆
Bb major				☆	☆
Bb minor				☆	☆

Advanced Inversions 2

	Rolled	Both	Blocked	Both
C# major / Db major	R.H. L.H.	☆	R.H. L.H.	☆
Eb major	R.H. L.H.	☆	R.H. L.H.	☆
F# major / Gb major	R.H. L.H.	☆	R.H. L.H.	☆
G# major / Ab major	R.H. L.H.	☆	R.H. L.H.	☆
Bb major	R.H. L.H.	☆	R.H. L.H.	☆
C# minor / Db minor	R.H. L.H.	☆	R.H. L.H.	☆
D# minor / Eb minor	R.H. L.H.	☆	R.H. L.H.	☆
F# minor	R.H. L.H.	☆	R.H. L.H.	☆
G# minor / Ab minor	R.H. L.H.	☆	R.H. L.H.	☆
A# minor / Bb minor	R.H. L.H.	☆	R.H. L.H.	☆

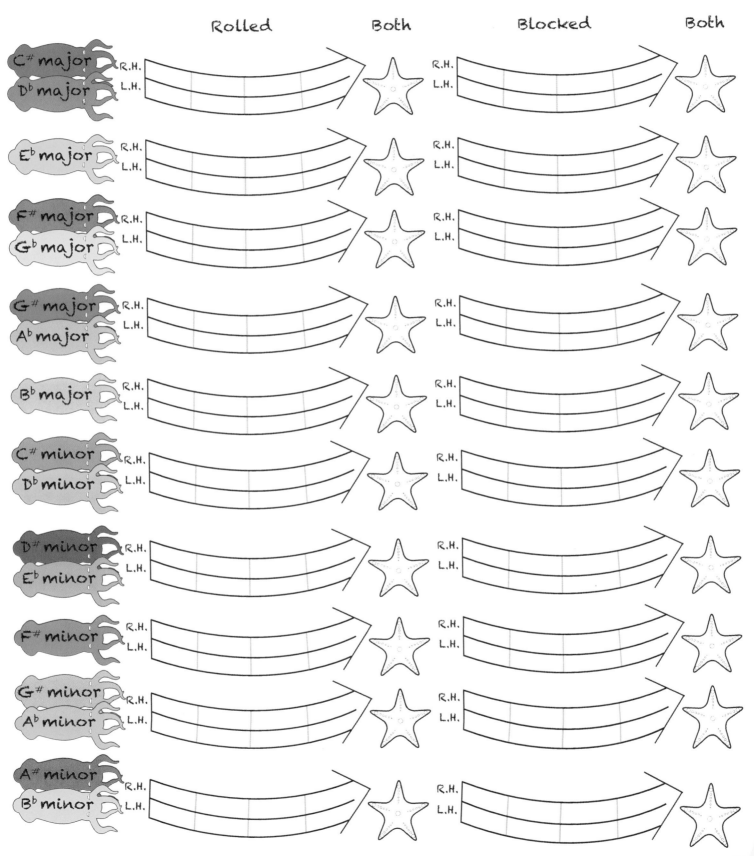

Major Scales 1

1 Octave

	R.H.	L.H.	Both
C major			
D major			
E major			
F major			
G major			
A major			
B major			

2 Octaves

	R.H.	L.H.	Both
C major			
D major			
E major			
F major			
G major			
A major			
B major			

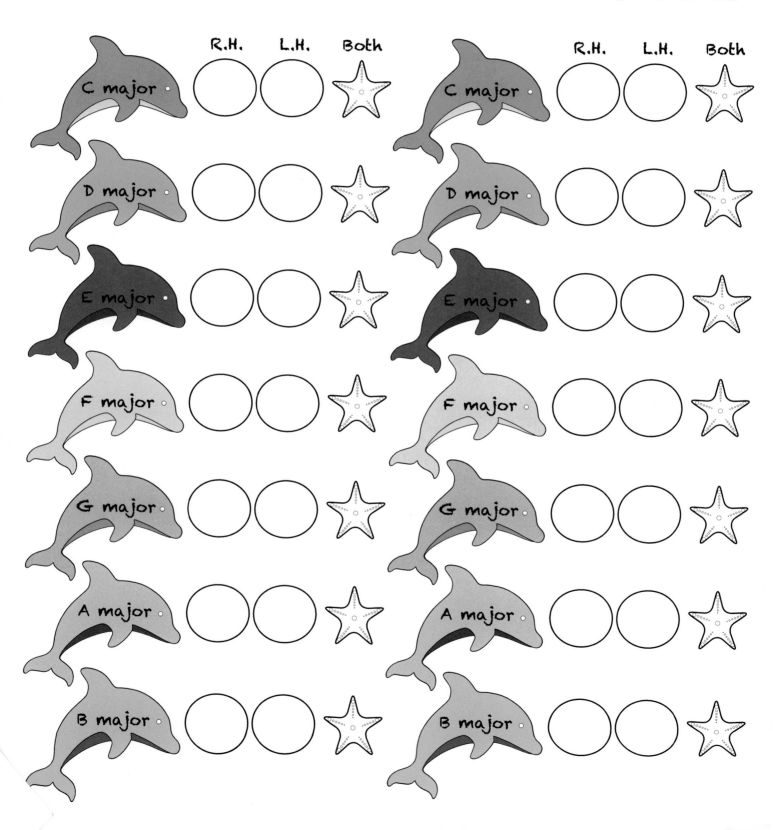

Write them out

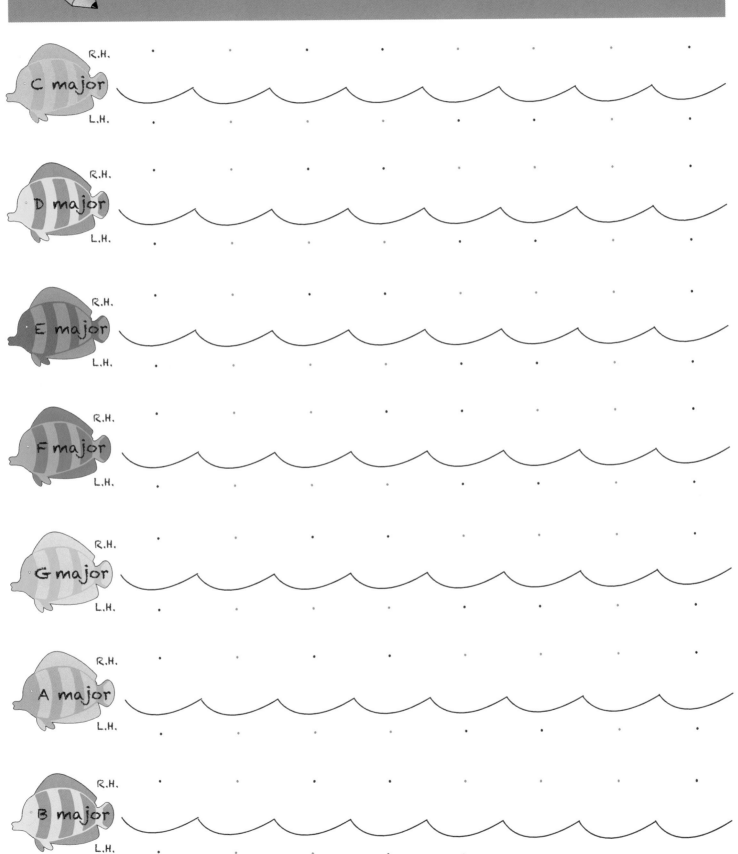

R.H.
C major
L.H.

R.H.
D major
L.H.

R.H.
E major
L.H.

R.H.
F major
L.H.

R.H.
G major
L.H.

R.H.
A major
L.H.

R.H.
B major
L.H.

Major Scales 2

1 Octave

	R.H.	L.H.	Both
$C^\#$ major			
D^b major			
E^b major			
$F^\#$ major			
G^b major			
A^b major			
B^b major			

2 Octaves

	R.H.	L.H.	Both
$C^\#$ major			
D^b major			
E^b major			
$F^\#$ major			
G^b major			
A^b major			
B^b major			

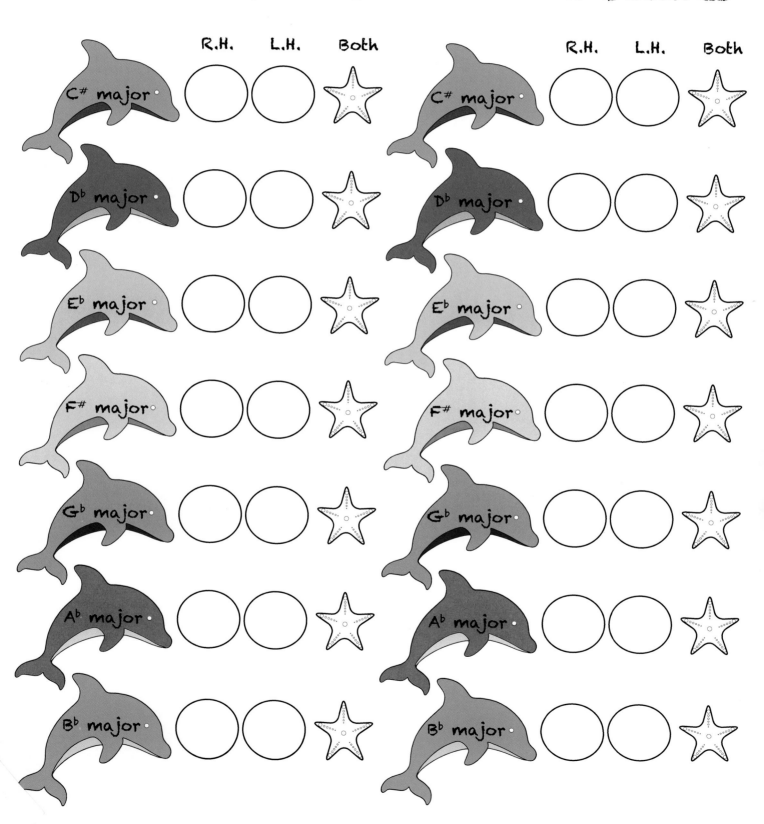

Write them out

R.H.

C♯ major

L.H.

R.H.

D♭ major

L.H.

R.H.

E♭ major

L.H.

R.H.

F♯ major

L.H.

R.H.

G♭ major

L.H.

R.H.

A♭ major

L.H.

R.H.

B♭ major

L.H.

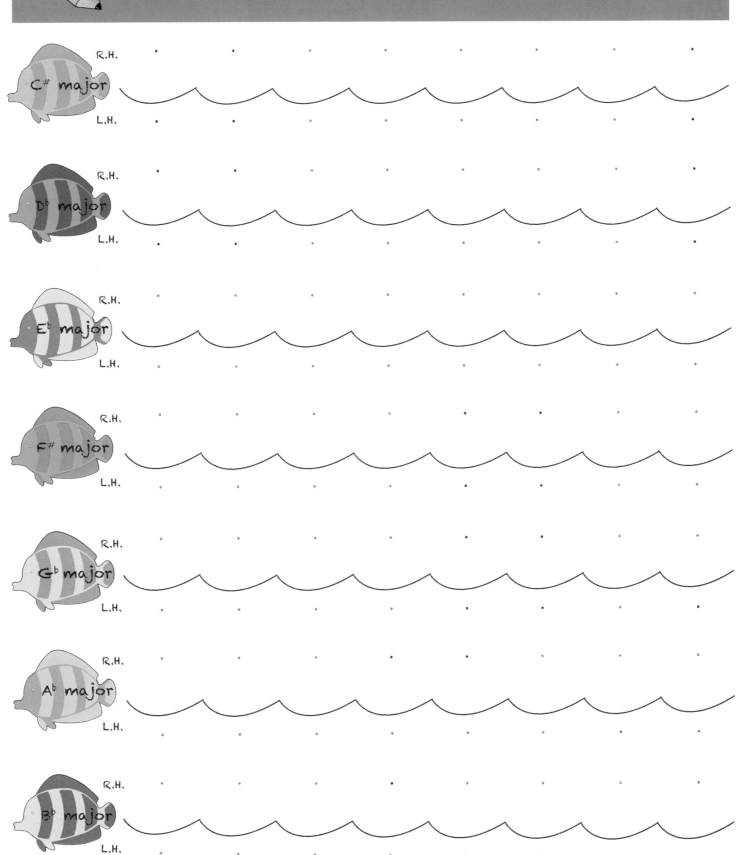

Natural Minor Scales 1

1 Octave	R.H.	L.H.	Both	2 Octaves	R.H.	L.H.	Both
C minor				C minor			
D minor				D minor			
E minor				E minor			
F minor				F minor			
G minor				G minor			
A minor				A minor			
B minor				B minor			

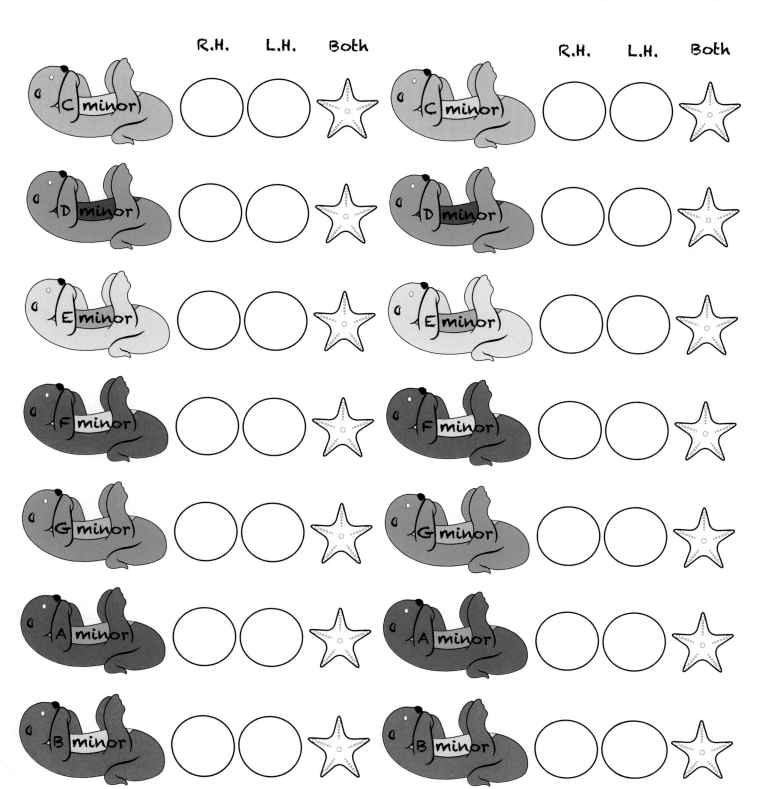

Write them out

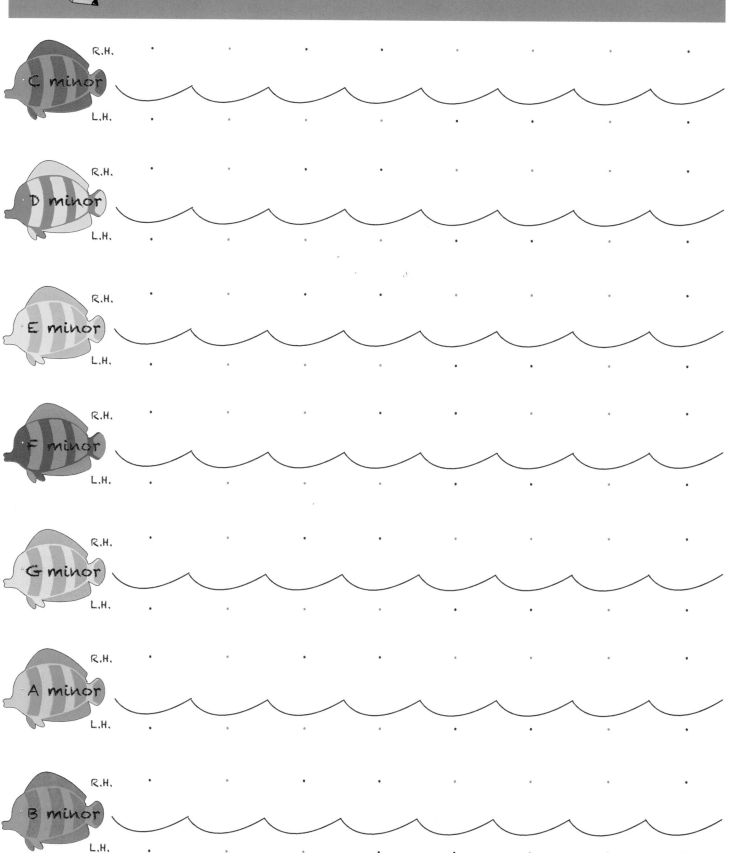

R.H.

C minor

L.H.

R.H.

D minor

L.H.

R.H.

E minor

L.H.

R.H.

F minor

L.H.

R.H.

G minor

L.H.

R.H.

A minor

L.H.

R.H.

B minor

L.H.

Natural Minor Scales 2

1 Octave

	R.H.	L.H.	Both
C# minor	◯	◯	☆
D# minor	◯	◯	☆
Eb minor	◯	◯	☆
F# minor	◯	◯	☆
G# minor	◯	◯	☆
Ab minor	◯	◯	☆
A# minor	◯	◯	☆
Bb minor	◯	◯	☆

2 Octaves

	R.H.	L.H.	Both
C# minor	◯	◯	☆
D# minor	◯	◯	☆
Eb minor	◯	◯	☆
F# minor	◯	◯	☆
G# minor	◯	◯	☆
Ab minor	◯	◯	☆
A# minor	◯	◯	☆
Bb minor	◯	◯	☆

Write them out

C$\sharp$ minor
R.H.
L.H.

D$\sharp$ minor
R.H.
L.H.

E$\flat$ minor
R.H.
L.H.

F$\sharp$ minor
R.H.
L.H.

G$\sharp$ minor
R.H.
L.H.

A$\flat$ minor
R.H.
L.H.

A$\sharp$ minor
R.H.
L.H.

B$\flat$ minor
R.H.
L.H.

Harmonic minor Scales 1

	1 Octave			2 Octaves			
	R.H.	L.H.	Both		R.H.	L.H.	Both
C minor				C minor			
D minor				D minor			
E minor				E minor			
F minor				F minor			
G minor				G minor			
A minor				A minor			
B minor				B minor			

Write them out

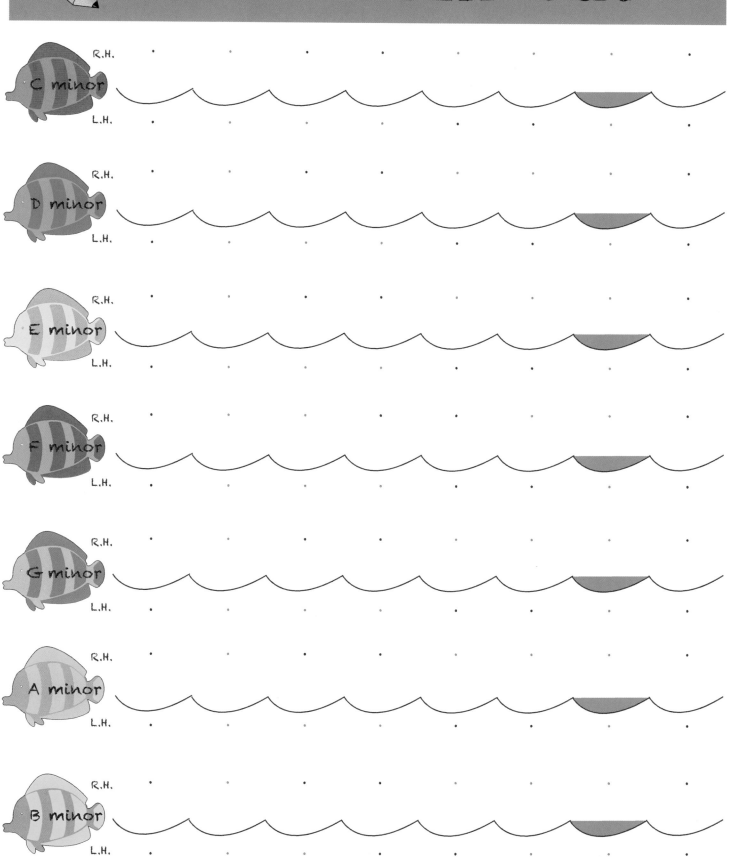

R.H.
C minor
L.H.

R.H.
D minor
L.H.

R.H.
E minor
L.H.

R.H.
F minor
L.H.

R.H.
G minor
L.H.

R.H.
A minor
L.H.

R.H.
B minor
L.H.

Harmonic Scales 2

	1 Octave			2 Octaves			
	R.H.	L.H.	Both		R.H.	L.H.	Both
C♯ minor				C♯ minor			
D♯ minor				D♯ minor			
E♭ minor				E♭ minor			
F♯ minor				F♯ minor			
G♯ minor				G♯ minor			
A♭ minor				A♭ minor			
A♯ minor				A♯ minor			
B♭ minor				B♭ minor			

Write them out

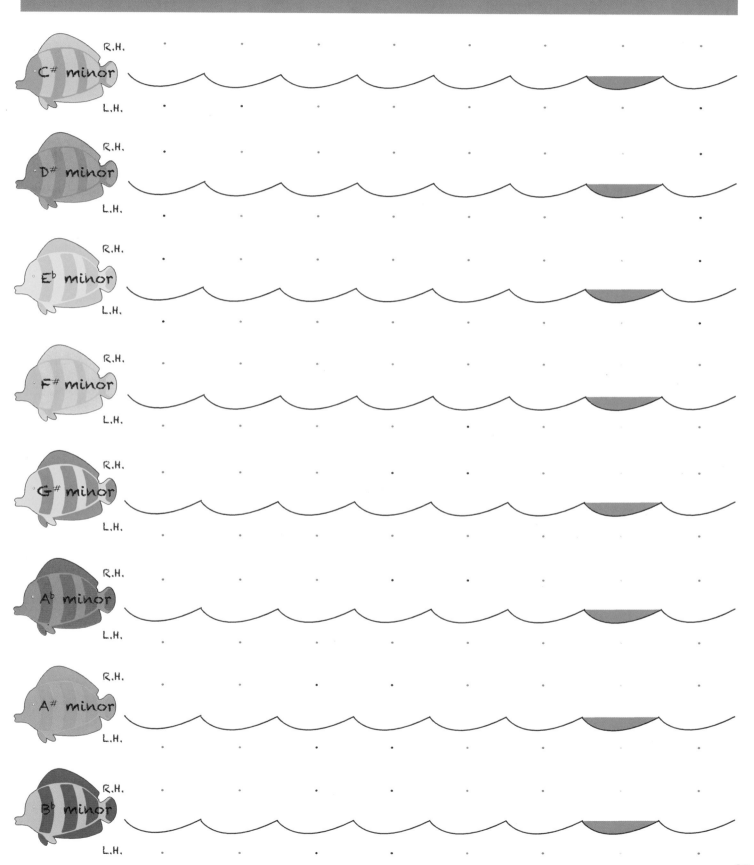

R.H.
C♯ minor
L.H.

R.H.
D♯ minor
L.H.

R.H.
E♭ minor
L.H.

R.H.
F♯ minor
L.H.

R.H.
G♯ minor
L.H.

R.H.
A♭ minor
L.H.

R.H.
A♯ minor
L.H.

R.H.
B♭ minor
L.H.

Melodic Scales 1

1 Octave

	R.H.	L.H.	Both
C minor			
D minor			
E minor			
F minor			
G minor			
A minor			
B minor			

2 Octaves

	R.H.	L.H.	Both
C minor			
D minor			
E minor			
F minor			
G minor			
A minor			
B minor			

Write them out

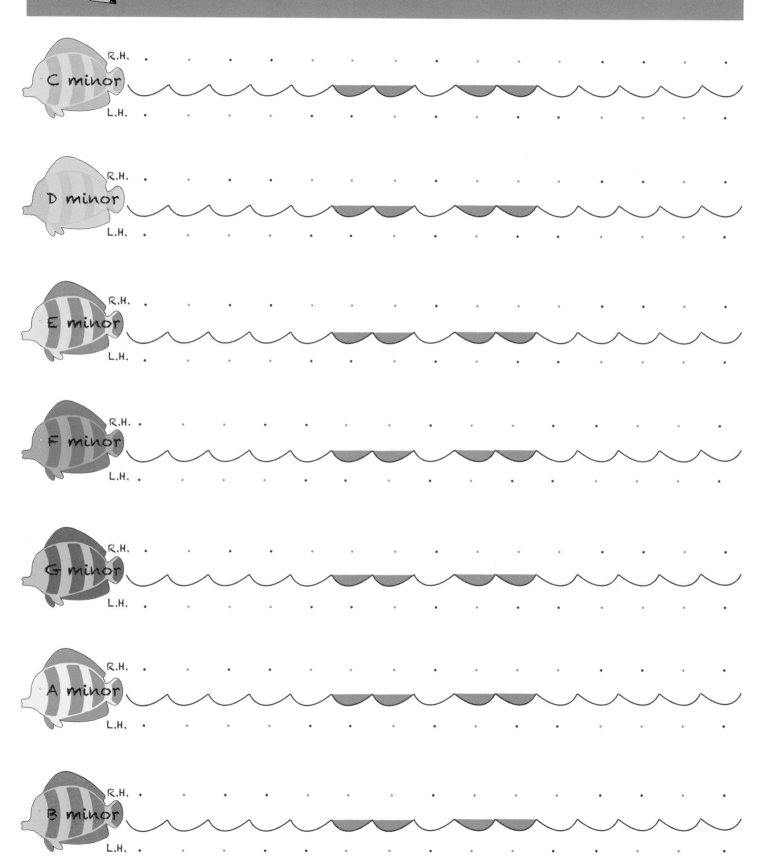

C minor

R.H.

L.H.

D minor

R.H.

L.H.

E minor

R.H.

L.H.

F minor

R.H.

L.H.

G minor

R.H.

L.H.

A minor

R.H.

L.H.

B minor

R.H.

L.H.

Melodic Scales 2

	1 Octave			2 Octaves		
	R.H.	L.H.	Both	R.H.	L.H.	Both
C# minor						
D# minor						
E♭ minor						
F# minor						
G# minor						
A♭ minor						
A# minor						
B♭ minor						

Write them out

R.H.
$C^{\#}$ minor
L.H.

R.H.
$D^{\#}$ minor
L.H.

R.H.
$E^{\flat}$ minor
L.H.

R.H.
$F^{\#}$ minor
L.H.

R.H.
$G^{\#}$ minor
L.H.

R.H.
$A^{\flat}$ minor
L.H.

R.H.
$A^{\#}$ minor
L.H.

R.H.
$B^{\flat}$ minor
L.H.

Chord Progressions 1

Are there any sharps or flats?	I	ii	iii	IV	V	vi	vii°
C major							
D major							
E major							
F major							
G major							
A major							
B major							

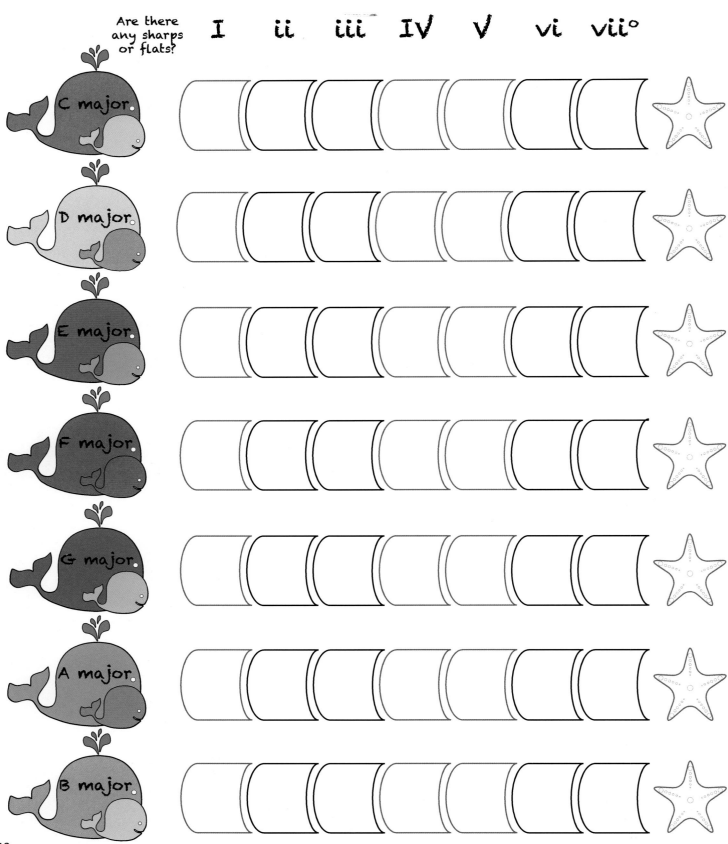

Chord Progressions 2

	Are there any sharps or flats?	i	ii°	III	iv	v	VI	VII
C minor								
D minor								
E minor								
F minor								
G minor								
A minor								
B minor								

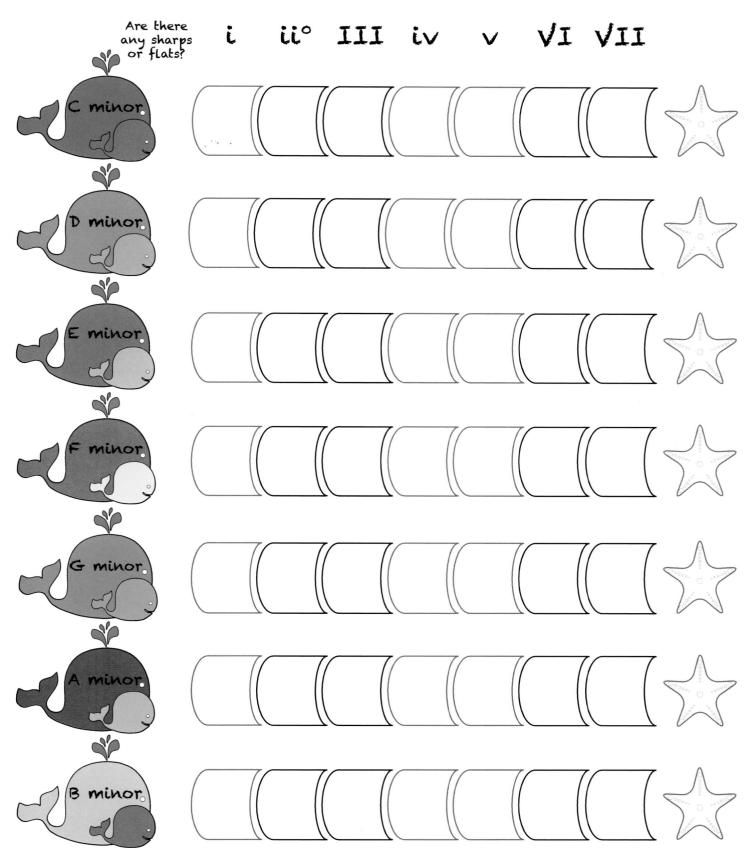

Chord Progressions 3

	What are the sharps or flats?	I	ii	iii	IV	V	vi	vii°
C# major								
D♭ major								
E♭ major								
F# major								
G♭ major								
A♭ major								
B♭ major								

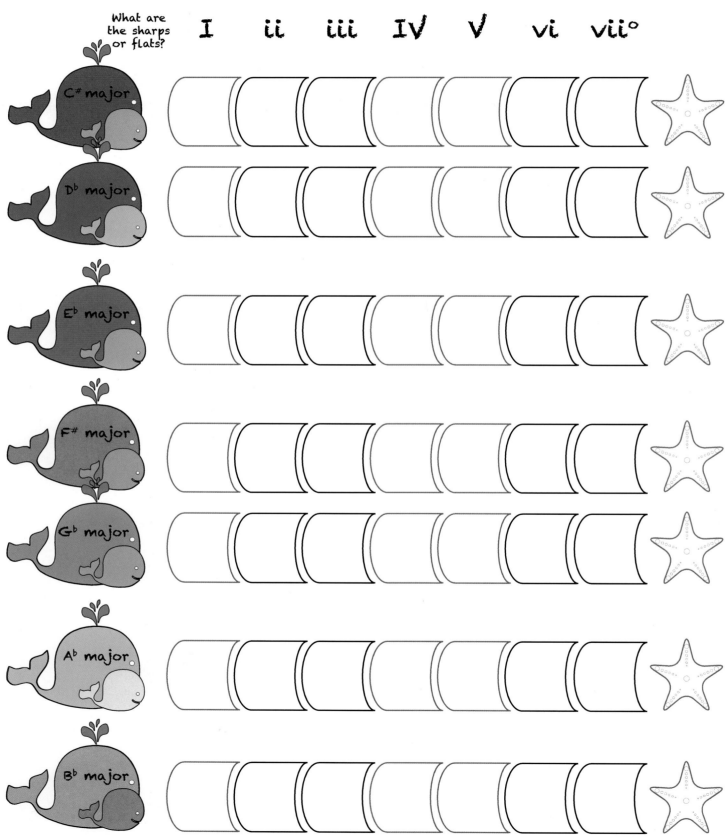

Chord Progressions 4

What are the sharps or flats?	i	ii°	III	iv	v	VI	VII
C# minor							
D# minor							
E♭ minor							
F# minor							
G# minor							
A♭ minor							
A# minor							
B♭ minor							

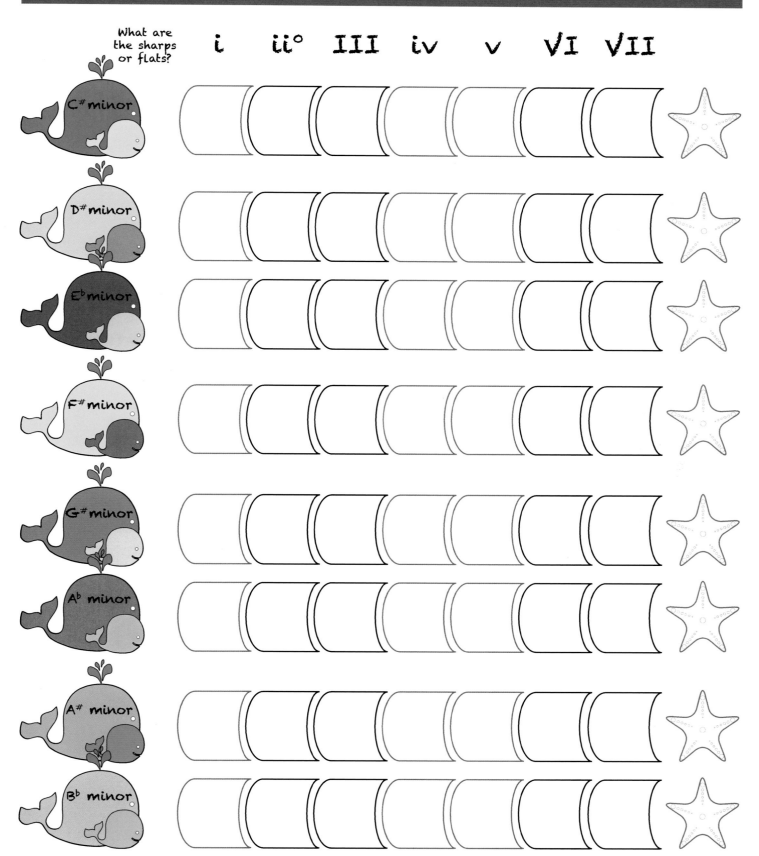

Identifying Intervals

1. A unison goes from a SPACE to a __________ OR a LINE to a __________

Circle all the unisons below

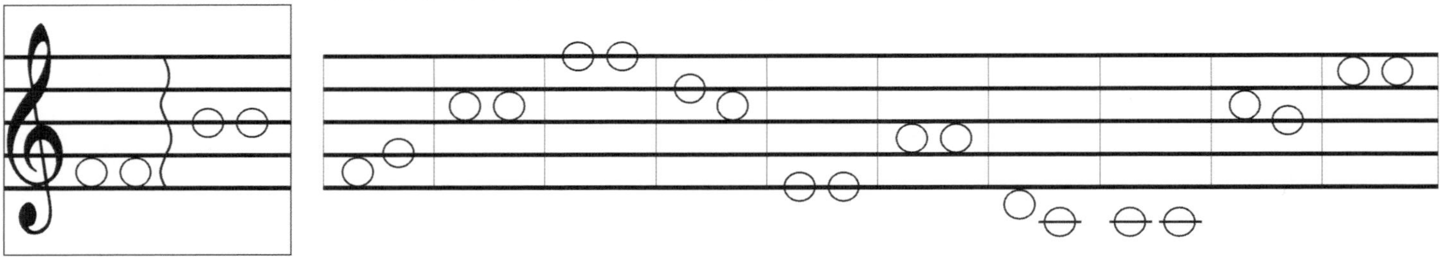

2. A second goes from a SPACE to a __________ OR a LINE to a __________

Circle all the seconds below

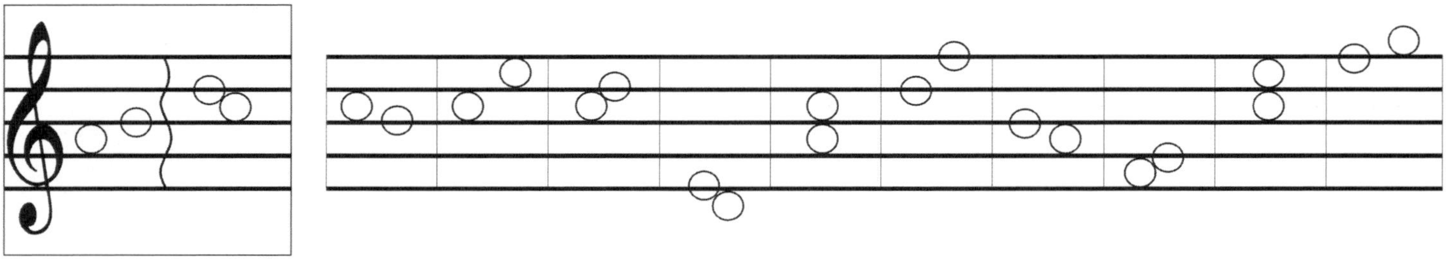

3. A third goes from a SPACE to a __________ OR a LINE to a __________

Circle all the thirds below

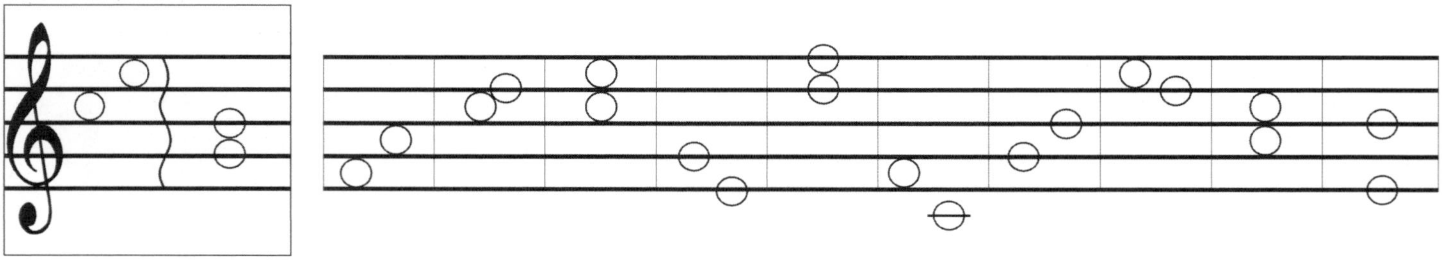

4. A fourth goes from a SPACE to a __________ OR a LINE to a __________

Circle all the fourths below

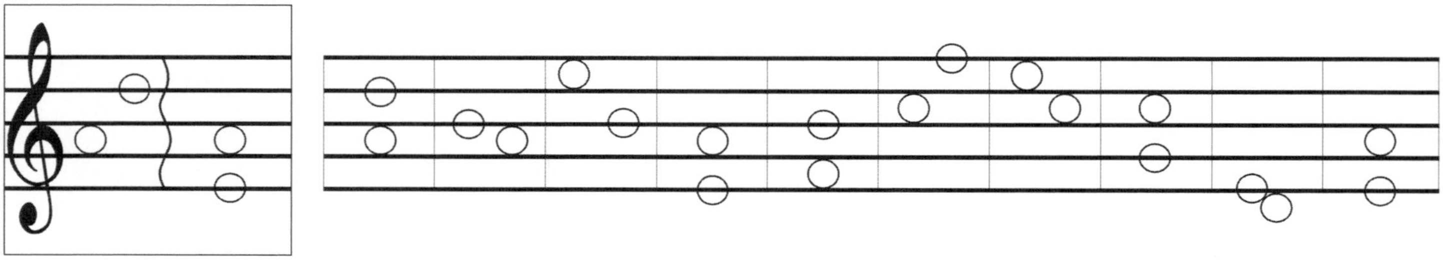

5 A fifth goes from a SPACE to a ____________ OR a LINE to a ____________

Circle all the fifths below

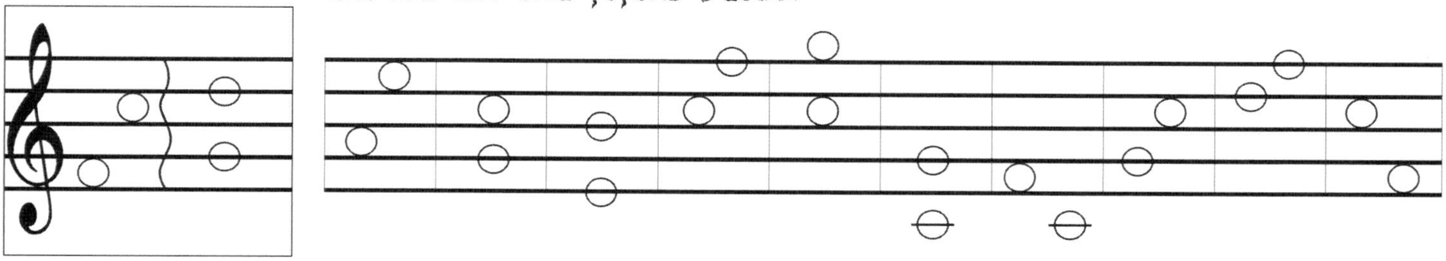

6 A sixth goes from a SPACE to a ____________ OR a LINE to a ____________

Circle all the sixths below

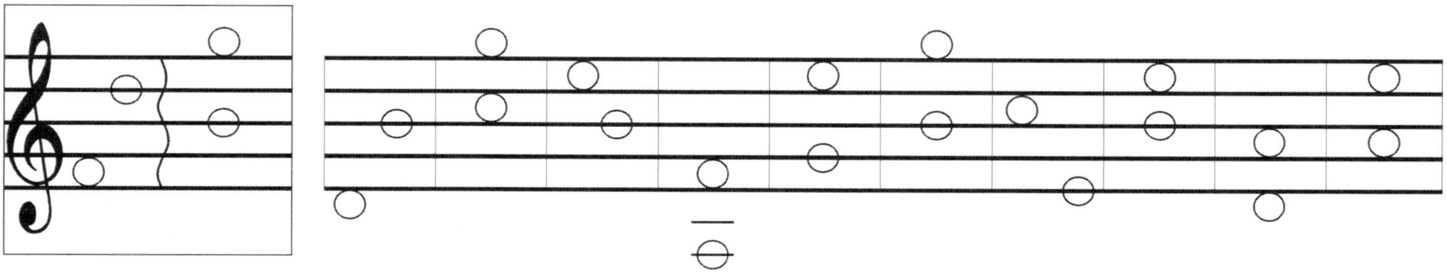

7 A seventh goes from a SPACE to a ____________ OR a LINE to a ____________

Circle all the sevenths below

8 An octave goes from a SPACE to a ____________ OR a LINE to a ____________

Circle all the octaves below

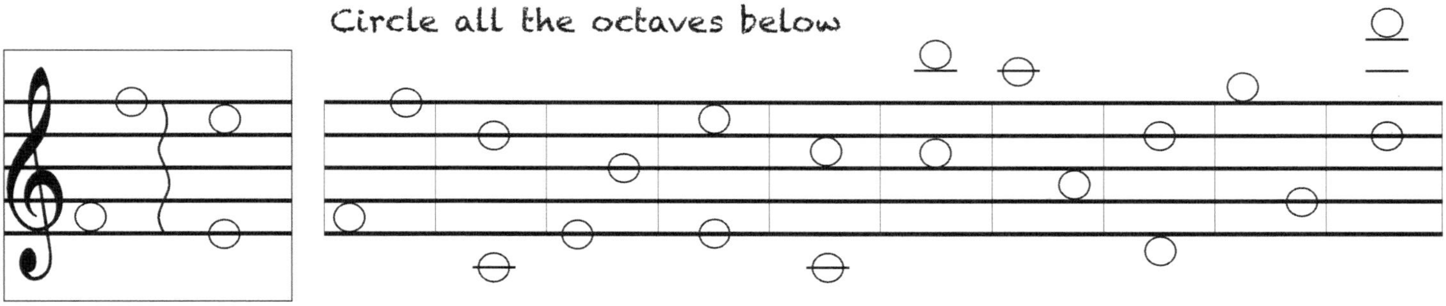

Intervals: Unisons

1. Choose a clef (Treble or Bass)
2. Draw a note in every measure
3. No need to fill in arrows for unisons
4. Draw the second note (beside the first note)
5. Play it on the piano!

1

↑or↓	N	O		A	R	R	O	W	S	!

2

↑or↓	N	O		A	R	R	O	W	S	!

3

↑or↓	N	O		A	R	R	O	W	S	!

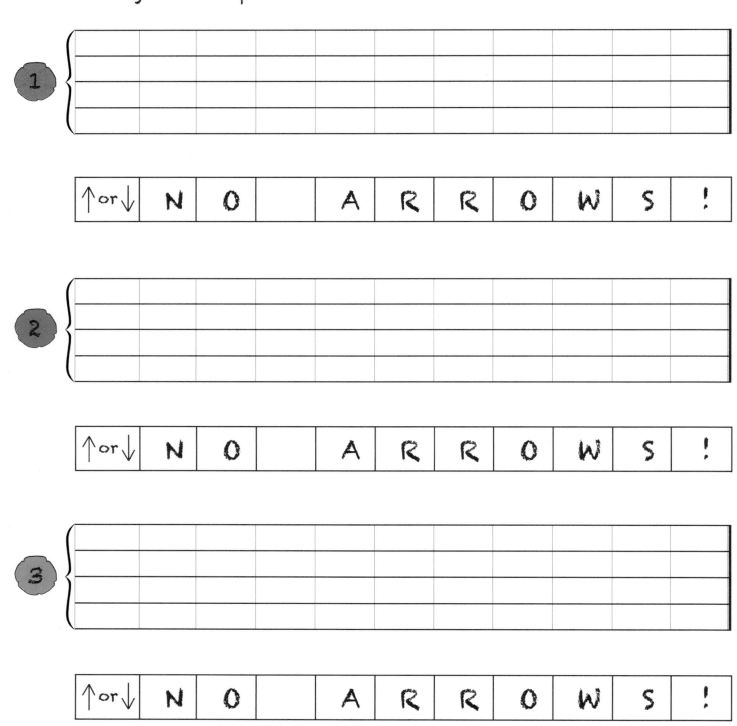

Intervals: Seconds

1. Choose a clef (Treble or Bass)
2. Draw a note in every measure
3. Fill in arrows (up or down)
4. Draw the second note (according to the arrows)
5. Play it on the piano!

1

↑ or ↓										

2

↑ or ↓										

3

↑ or ↓										

Intervals: Thirds

1. Choose a clef (Treble or Bass)
2. Draw a note in every measure
3. Fill in arrows (up or down)
4. Draw the second note (according to the arrows)
5. Play it on the piano!

1

↑ or ↓										

2

↑ or ↓										

3

↑ or ↓										

Intervals: Fourths

1. Choose a clef (Treble or Bass)
2. Draw a note in every measure
3. Fill in arrows (up or down)
4. Draw the second note (according to the arrows)
5. Play it on the piano!

1

↑or↓										

2

↑or↓										

3

↑or↓										

Intervals: Fifths

1. Choose a clef (Treble or Bass)
2. Draw a note in every measure
3. Fill in arrows (up or down)
4. Draw the second note (according to the arrows)
5. Play it on the piano!

1

↑ or ↓										

2

↑ or ↓										

3

↑ or ↓										

Intervals: Sixths

1. Choose a clef (Treble or Bass)
2. Draw a note in every measure
3. Fill in arrows (up or down)
4. Draw the second note (according to the arrows)
5. Play it on the piano!

1

↑ or ↓										

2

↑ or ↓										

3

↑ or ↓										

Intervals: Sevenths

1. Choose a clef (Treble or Bass)
2. Draw a note in every measure
3. Fill in arrows (up or down)
4. Draw the second note (according to the arrows)
5. Play it on the piano!

1

↑or↓										

2

↑or↓										

3

↑or↓										

Intervals: Octaves

1. Choose a clef (Treble or Bass)
2. Draw a note in every measure
3. Fill in arrows (up or down)
4. Draw the second note (according to the arrows)
5. Play it on the piano!

1

↑ or ↓										

2

↑ or ↓										

3

↑ or ↓										

Interval Index

	Ascending	Descending
m2	Jaws Pink Panther Ave Maria (Bach)	Fur Elise (Beethoven) Joy To the World Symphony No. 40 (Mozart) O Little Town of Bethlehem
M2	Happy Birthday Do Re Mi / Do, a Deer Silent Night Rudolph the Red Nosed Reindeer Frere Jacques	Mary Had a Little Lamb The First Noel Three Blind Mice Yesterday (Beatles) Toccata and Fugue in D minor (Bach)
m3	Greensleeves Lullaby (Brahms) So Long, Farewell (Sound of Music) Edelweiss (Sound of Music)	Hey Jude (Beatles) Frosty, the Snowman Star Spangled Banner This Old Man
M3	Oh When the Saints Kum Ba Yah Spring (Vivaldi)	5th Symphony (Beethoven) Dorbell (ding dong) Summertime (Gershwin) Swing Low, Sweet Chariot
P4	Amazing Grace Here Comes the Bride Oh Christmas Tree Hark the Herald Angels Sing We Wish You a Merry Christmas	Oh, Come All Ye Faithful I've Been Working on the Railroad Eine Klein Nachtmusik (Mozart)
Tritone	The Simpsons Maria (West Side Story)	European Police Siren My Favorite Things (Sound of Music)
P5	Twinkle Twinkle Little Star ABC's Baa Baa Black Sheep My Favorite Things (Sound of Music)	Minuet in G (Bach) Swan Lake Suite (op. 20) Flinstones
m6	Because (Beatles) The Entertainer Love Story Grenade (Bruno Mars)	Love Story Five for Fighting (100 Years)
M6	My Bonnie Lies Over the Ocean NBC Chimes Dashing Through the Snow (Jingle Bells) Hush Little Baby It Came Upon a Midnight Clear	The Music of the Night (Phantom of the Opera) Il etait un petit navire La Cucaracha
m7	There's a Place for Us (West Side Story) Animals (Maroon 5)	White Christmas
M7	Don't Know Why (Norah Jones)	Have Yourself a Merry Little Christmas
Octave	Somewhere Over the Rainbow (Wizard of Oz) Let it Snow Take Me Out to the Ballgame Chestnuts Roasting on an Open Fire Clair de Lune (Debussy)	Alouette Yoddeling Song (Sound of Music)

Interval Song Chart

	Ascending	Descending
m2		
M2		
m3		
M3		
P4		
Tritone		
P5		
m6		
M6		
m7		
M7		
Octave		

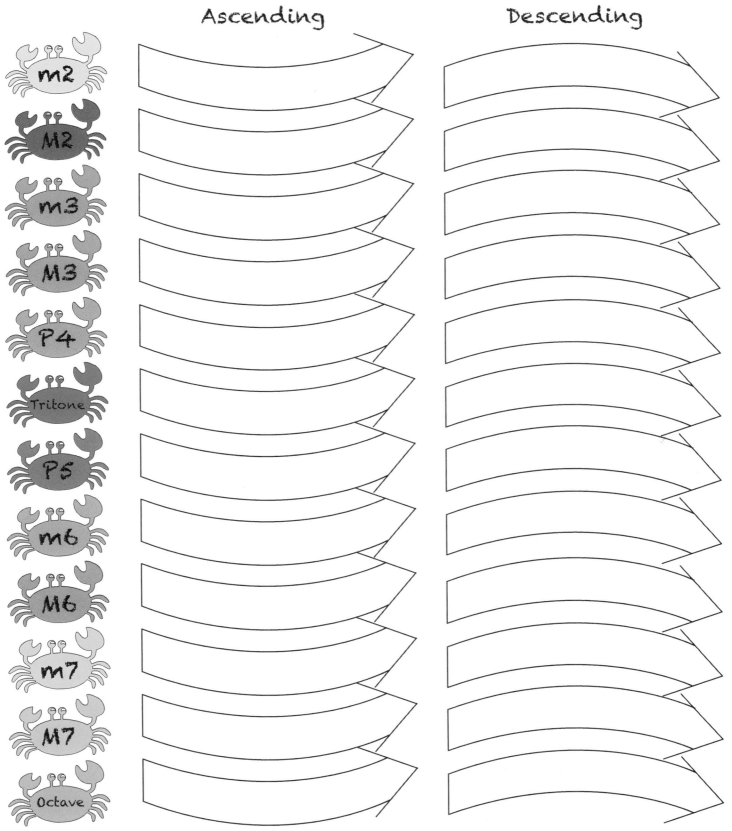

Melodic Ear Training 1

Ascending | Descending

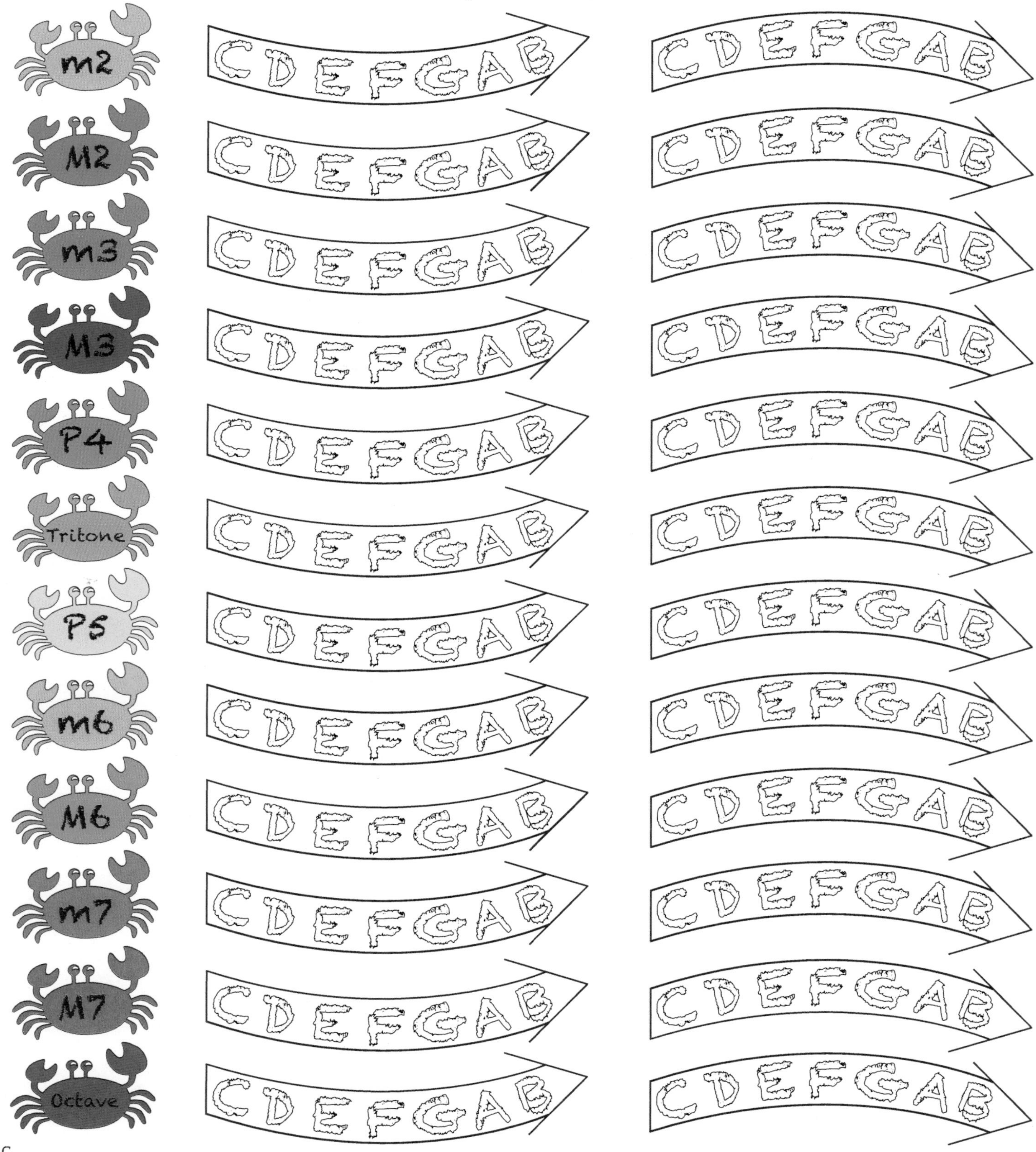

Melodic Ear Training 2

Ascending | Descending

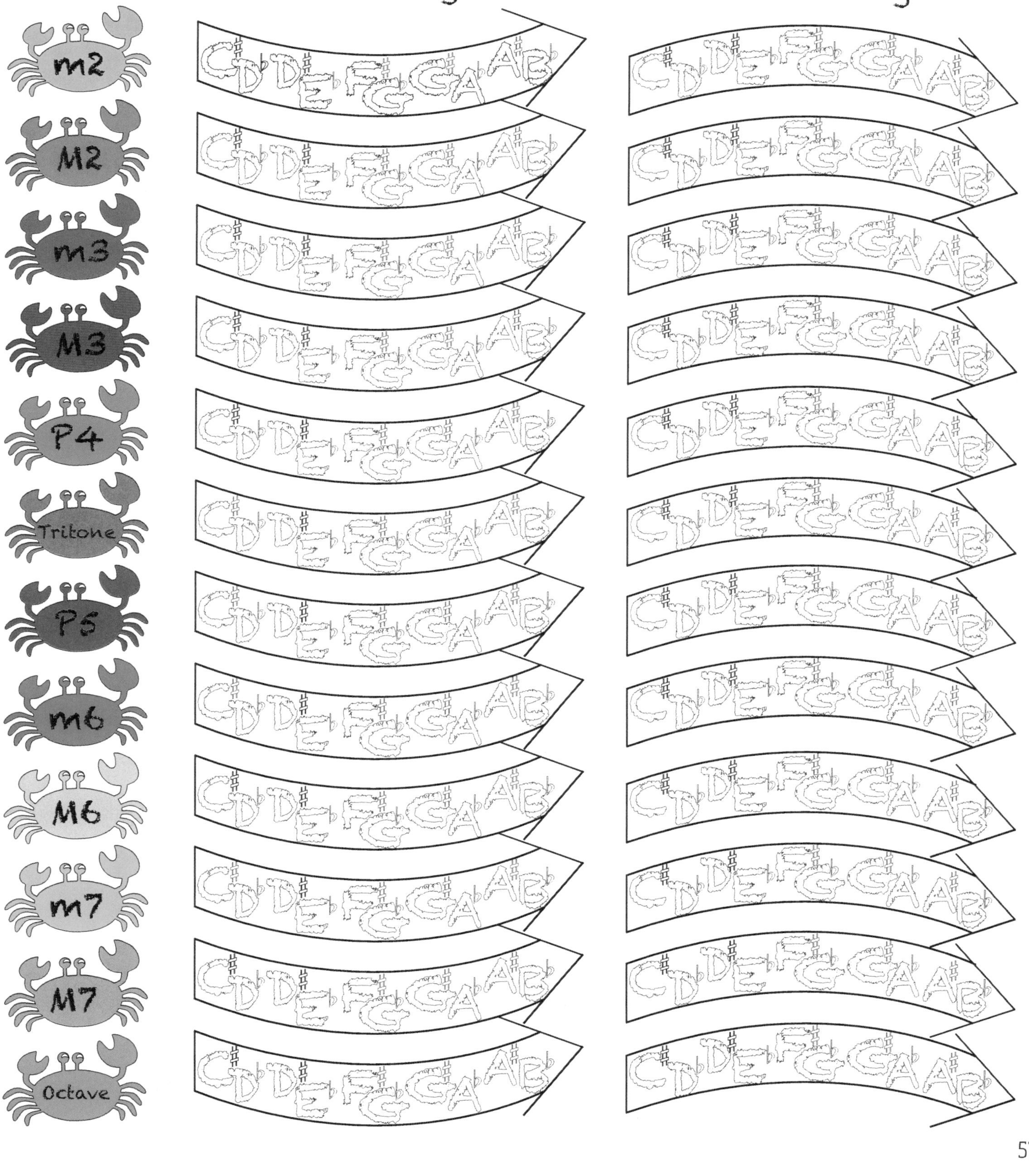

Melodic Ear Training 3

	C	D	E	F	G	A	B
m2							
M2							
m3							
M3							
P4							
Tritone							
P5							
m6							
M6							
m7							
M7							
Octave							

Melodic Ear Training 4

	C#Db	D#Eb	F#Gb	G#Ab	A#Bb
m2					
M2					
m3					
M3					
P4					
Tritone					
P5					
m6					
M6					
m7					
M7					
Octave					

Harmonic Ear Training 1

m2 C · D · E · F · G · A · B

M2 C · D · E · F · G · A · B

m3 C · D · E · F · G · A · B

M3 C · D · E · F · G · A · B

P4 C · D · E · F · G · A · B

Tritone C · D · E · F · G · A · B

P5 C · D · E · F · G · A · B

m6 C · D · E · F · G · A · B

M6 C · D · E · F · G · A · B

m7 C · D · E · F · G · A · B

M7 C · D · E · F · G · A · B

Octave C · D · E · F · G · A · B

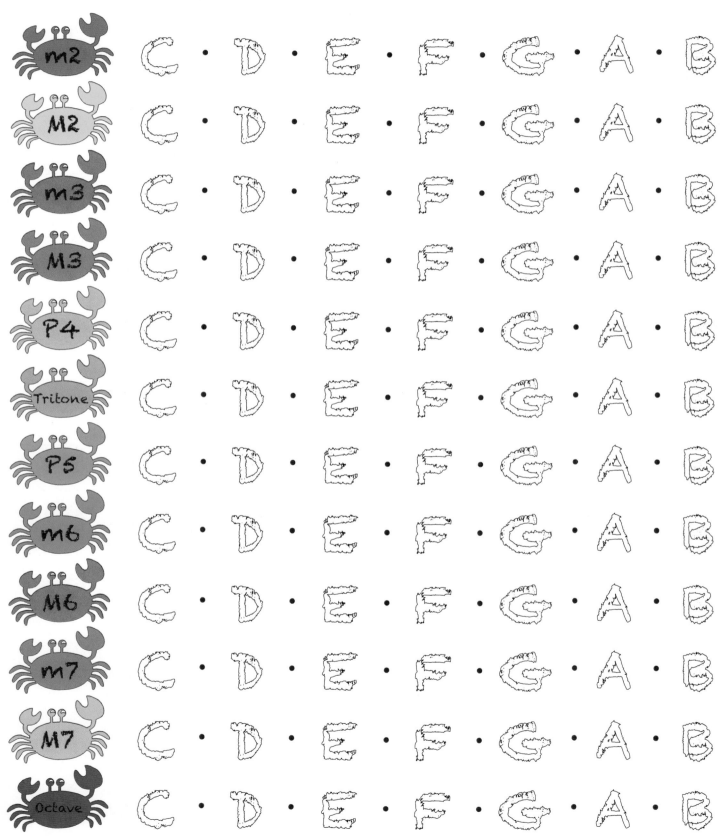

Harmonic Ear Training 2

m2 C#Db · D#Eb · F#Gb · G#Ab · A#Bb

M2 C#Db · D#Eb · F#Gb · G#Ab · A#Bb

m3 C#Db · D#Eb · F#Gb · G#Ab · A#Bb

M3 C#Db · D#Eb · F#Gb · G#Ab · A#Bb

P4 C#Db · D#Eb · F#Gb · G#Ab · A#Bb

Tritone C#Db · D#Eb · F#Gb · G#Ab · A#Bb

P5 C#Db · D#Eb · F#Gb · G#Ab · A#Bb

m6 C#Db · D#Eb · F#Gb · G#Ab · A#Bb

M6 C#Db · D#Eb · F#Gb · G#Ab · A#Bb

m7 C#Db · D#Eb · F#Gb · G#Ab · A#Bb

M7 C#Db · D#Eb · F#Gb · G#Ab · A#Bb

Octave C#Db · D#Eb · F#Gb · G#Ab · A#Bb

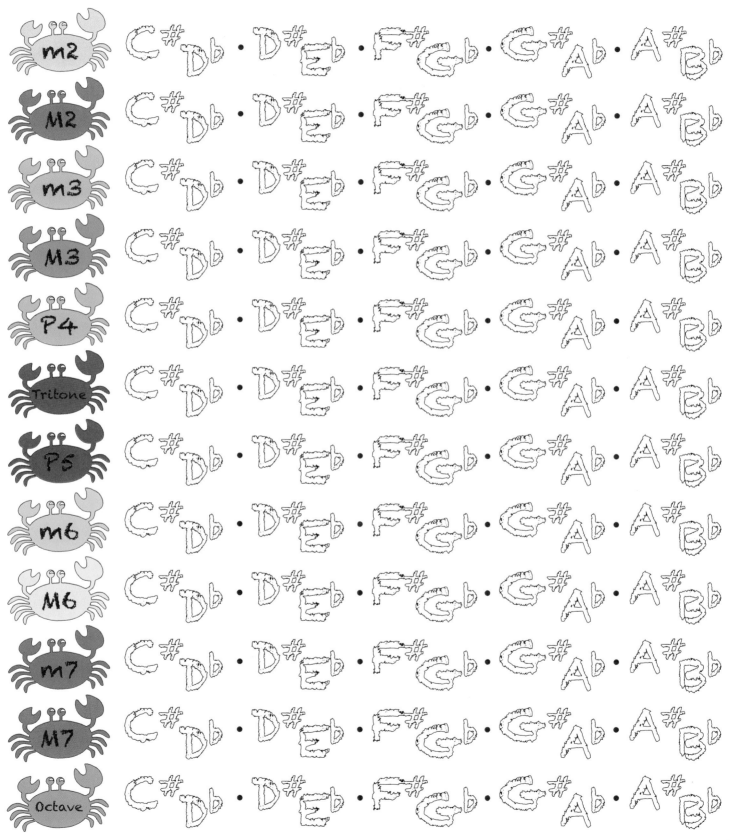

Harmonic Ear Training 3

	C	D	E	F	G	A	B
m2	△	△	△	△	△	△	△
M2	△	△	△	△	△	△	△
m3	△	△	△	△	△	△	△
M3	△	△	△	△	△	△	△
P4	△	△	△	△	△	△	△
Tritone	△	△	△	△	△	△	△
P5	△	△	△	△	△	△	△
m6	△	△	△	△	△	△	△
M6	△	△	△	△	△	△	△
m7	△	△	△	△	△	△	△
M7	△	△	△	△	△	△	△
Octave	△	△	△	△	△	△	△

Harmonic Ear Training 4

	C#D♭	D#E♭	F#G♭	G#A♭	A#B♭
m2					
M2					
m3					
M3					
P4					
Tritone					
P5					
m6					
M6					
m7					
M7					
Octave					

Scale Degrees 1

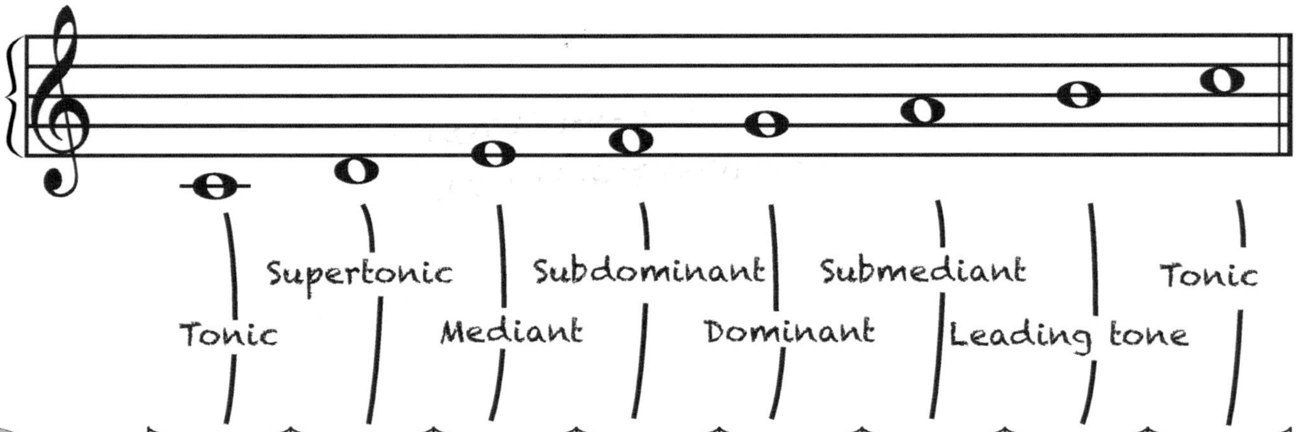

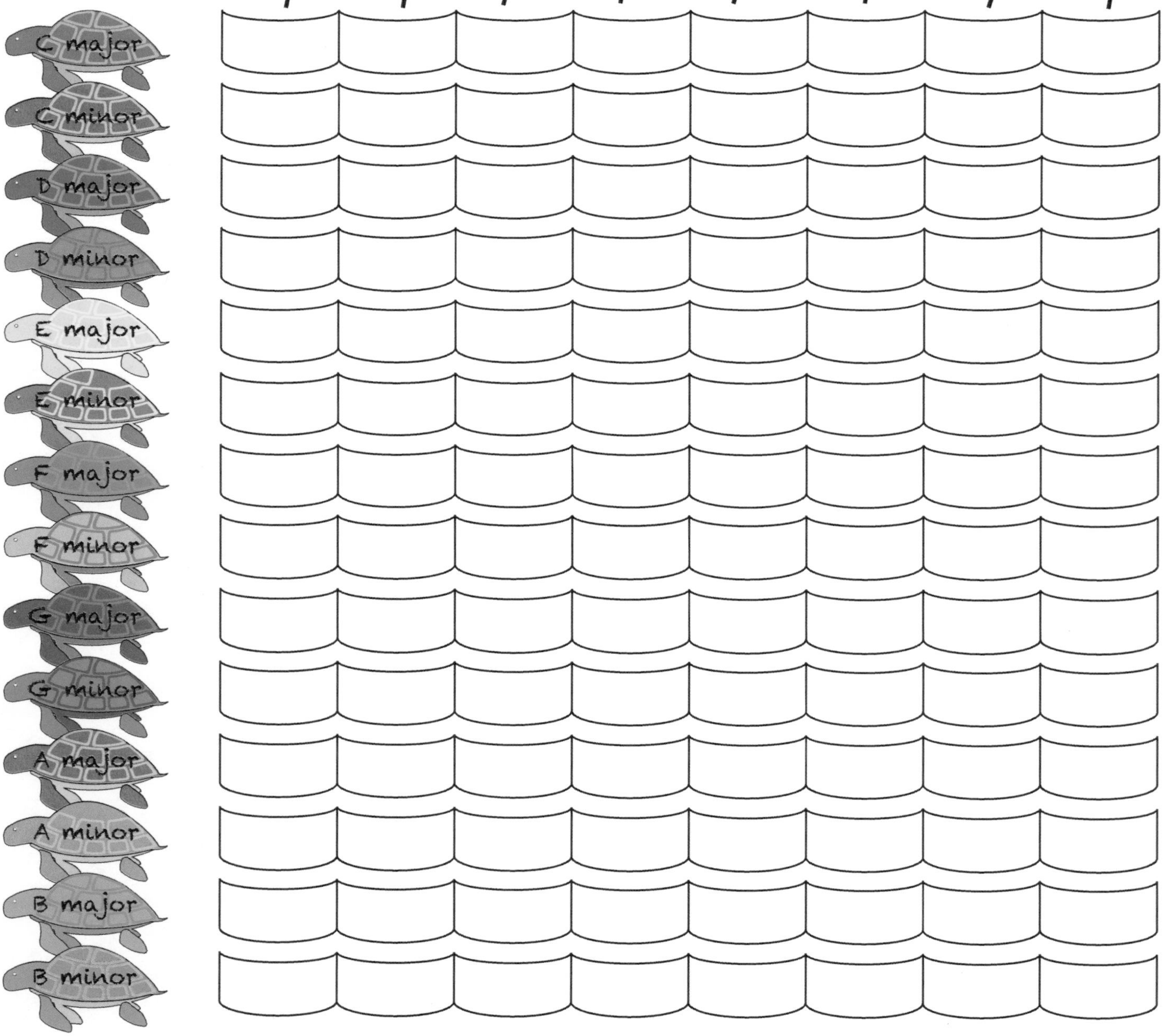

Scale Degrees 2

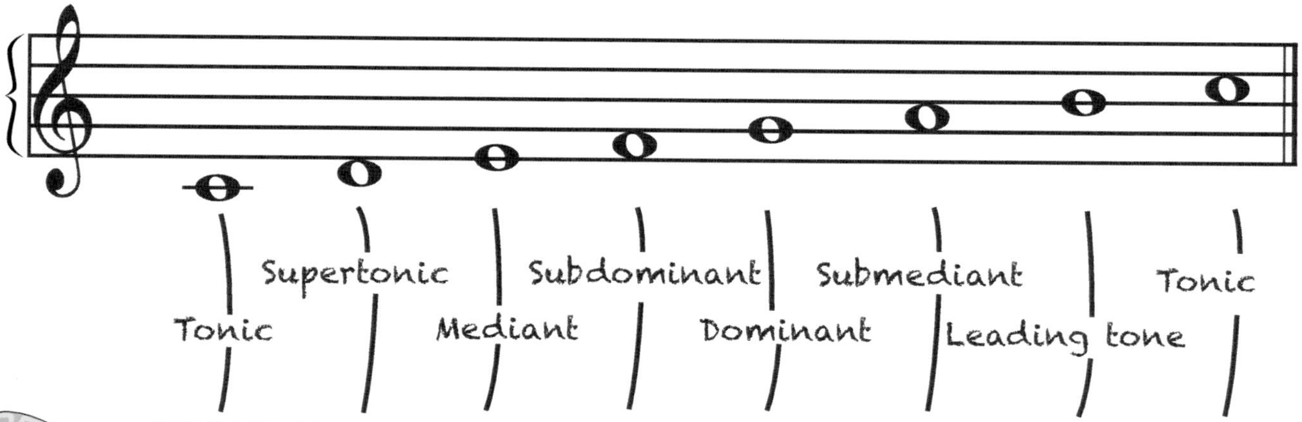

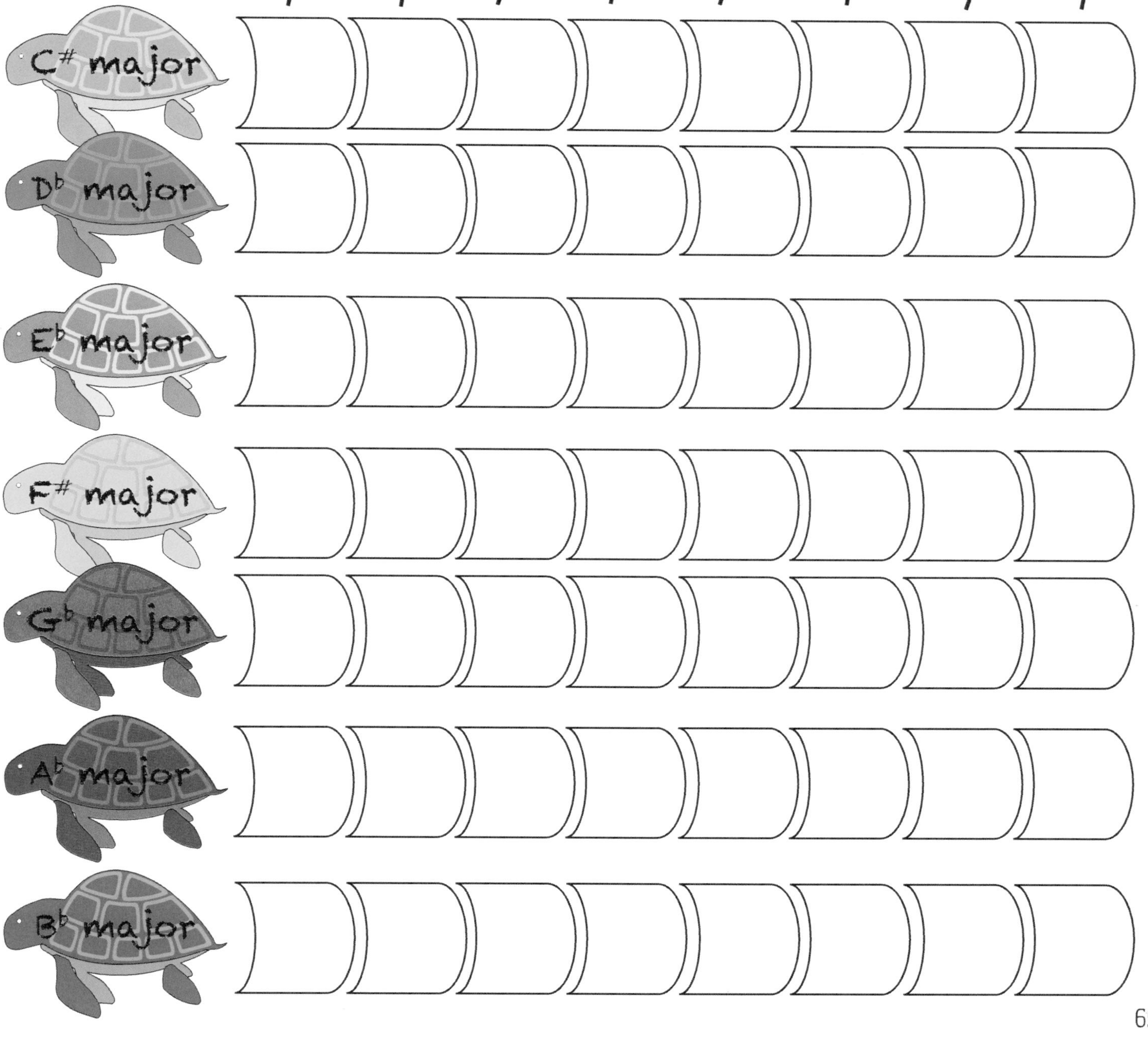

Scale Degrees 3

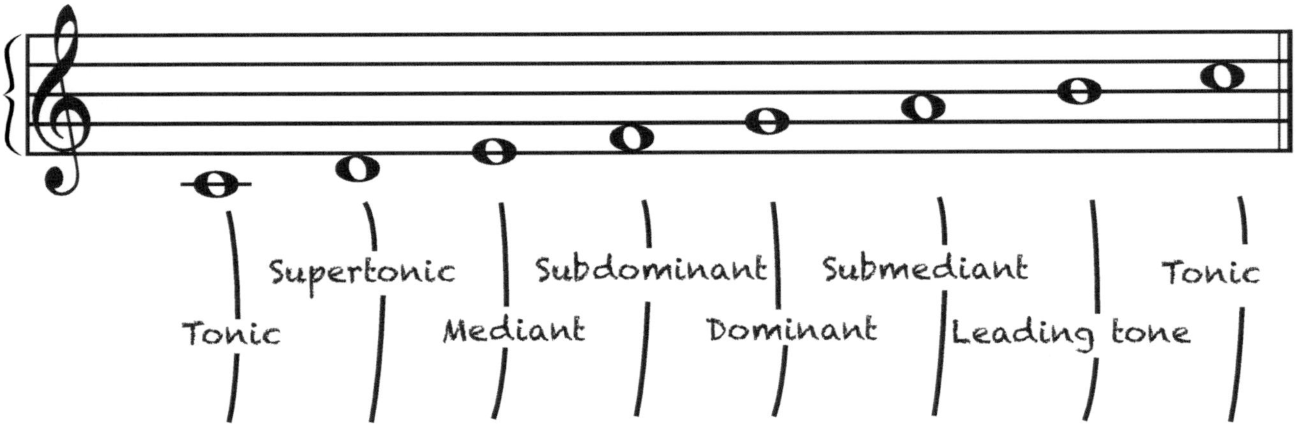

Sight Reading

1

2

3

4

5

6

7

8

9

10

11

12

13

14

15

16

17

18

19

20

21

22

23

24

25

26

27

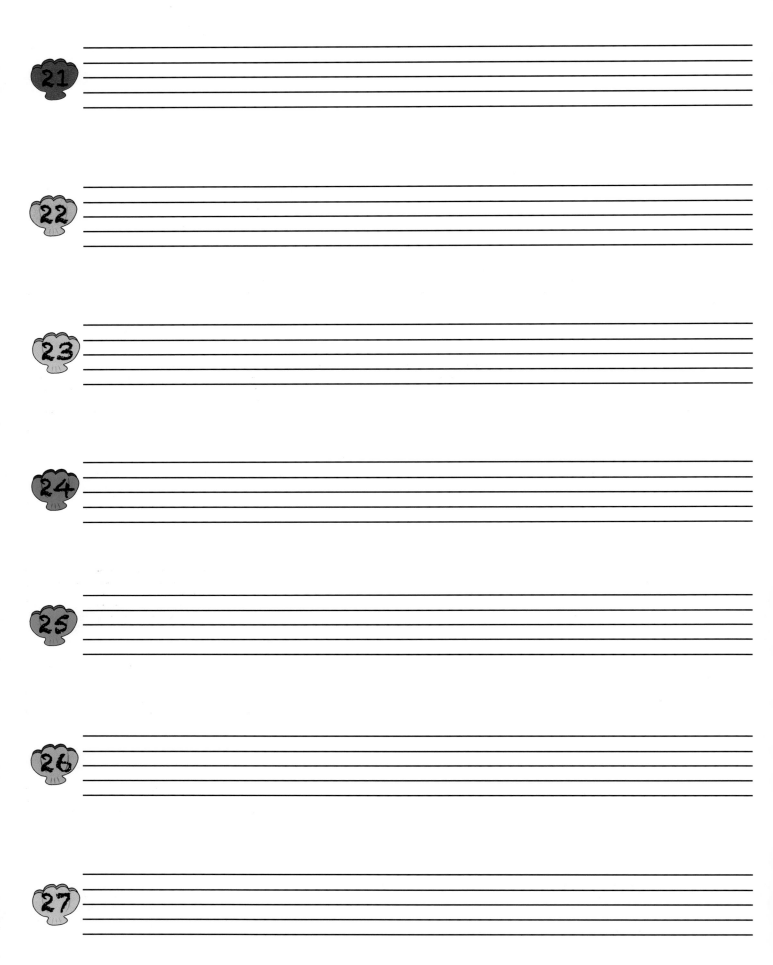

Staff Paper

Improvisation

I can improvise in the following keys:

C major
D major
E major
F major
G major
A major
B major

C minor
D minor
E minor
F minor
G minor
A minor
B minor

C# major
Db major
Eb major
F# major
Gb major
Ab major
Bb major

C# minor
D# minor
Eb minor
F# minor
G# minor
Ab minor
A# minor
Bb minor

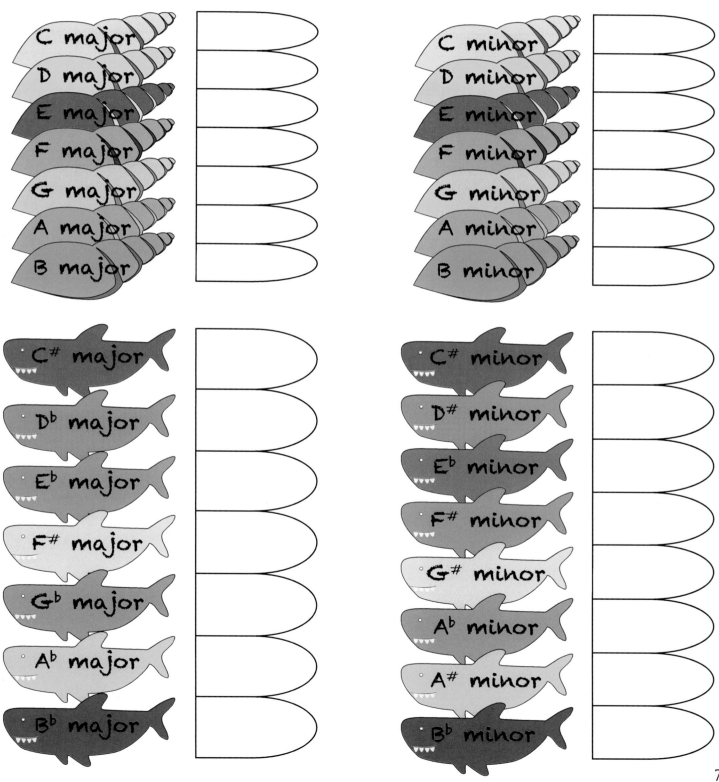

Time Chart

FLASH CARDS			
Date	Time(s)		

CHORD ROLLS Maj+Min.			
Date	Time(s)		

Date	What are you timing?	Time(s)

Online resources available at
www.TheCascadeMethod.com
www.CascadeMelody.com
www.NoteMatchOfficial.com

Production: Tara O'Brien
Cover, Design and Illustrations:
Tara O'Brien & Thomas O'Brien
ISBN-13: 9781542387873
ISBN-10: 1542387876

Made in the USA
Coppell, TX
27 November 2019

12005258R00048